Development Interventions in Wollaita, 1960s-2000s
A Critical Review

FSS Monograph No. 4

Dessalegn Rahmato

fSS

Forum for Social Studies
Addis Ababa

ISBN 10: 99944-50-13-1
ISBN 13: 978-99944-50-13-8

Forum for Social Studies (FSS)
P.O. Box 25864 code 1000
Addis Ababa, Ethiopia
Email: fss@ethionet.et
Web: www.fssethiopia.org.et

Cover photos: courtesy of Action for Development

This monograph was published with the financial support of the Department for International Development (DFID, UK), the Embassy of Denmark, the Embassy of Ireland, the Royal Embassy of the Netherlands, and the Norwegian Church Aid.

Contents

List of Tables and Maps

Tables

Acknowledgements

This study was conceived and sponsored by three NGOs, namely, **Action for Development, Christian Aid,** and **Inter-Church Organization for Development Cooperation (ICCO)**, which have had a long association with Wollaita in one form or another. The latter two provide funding and other forms of assistance to NGOs running programs in rural communities. Action for Development is engaged in community based rural development in several Zones in the Southern Killil, and until it phased out its program at the end of 2004, it had a strong presence in Wollaita. The study that the three Organizations commissioned was aimed at initiating broad-based debate and dialogue about the development challenges facing Wollaita. I would like to thank all three for their support and cooperation during the preparation of the study and for allowing me to have the work published by FSS.

I would also like to thank all informants who generously gave us their time and provided valuable information and documents, especially government officials in Soddo, NGO staff in Addis Ababa and Soddo, peasants in Bolloso, Damot Gale and Kindo Koysha woredas and businessmen in Soddo, without whose cooperation this study would not have been completed.

Finally, I would like to acknowledge and thank my research assistant, Mellese Madda of Debub University, who diligently collected information useful to the study and conducted all the peasant interviews in the field.

Acronyms

AFD:	Action for Development
AMRC:	Arba Minch Rehabilitation Center
CCCE:	Children's Cross Connection Ethiopia
CRDA:	Christian Relief and Development Association
CSO (A):	Central Statistical Office (Authority)
DFED:	Department of Finance and Economic Development (Soddo)
DARD:	Department of Agriculture and Rural Development (Soddo)
DPPC:	Disaster Prevention and Preparedness Commission
EDRI:	Ethiopian Development Research Institute
EPRDF:	Ethiopian Peoples Revolutionary Democratic Front
FDRE:	Federal Democratic Government of Ethiopia
FGA:	Family Guidance Association (Soddo)
ICCO:	Inter-Church Organization for Development Cooperation
NCFSE:	New Coalition for Food Security in Ethiopia
MFT:	Mossy Foot Prevention & Treatment Association
NGO:	Non-Government Organization
RRC:	Relief and Rehabilitation Commission
SNNPR:	Southern Nations, Nationalities and Peoples' Region
WADU:	Wollaita Agricultural Development Unit
WDA:	Wollaita Development Association

Summary

This study examines the development interventions of the last four and half decades from the point of view of three key determinants of poverty and destitution, namely, population dynamics and land shortage, urbanization and commercialization, and livelihood diversification

Wollaita is one of the most thickly settled areas of the country, and in some places, the population density compares with that found in the highly overpopulated areas of south-east Asia. The complex impact of demographic pressure on natural resources and living space, poverty and income, farming systems, the ecological balance of the rural areas, and public health is quite obvious but has not been seriously examined. Wollaita is a land of micro-holdings. Partly as a result of population dynamics, partly because of the specific farming system of the area, per capita land holdings have always been small relative to other parts of the country. The evidence indicates, however, that family holdings have been growing smaller through the decades, and in recent years this has been compounded by growing landlessness especially among the young.

Over the last four and half decades, considerable effort has been made and immense resources invested in Wollaita by government, NGOs and other non-state actors. The achievements are by no means insignificant. Since the 1960s, when Wollaita was almost totally neglected, a good deal of investment in basic infrastructure, social services, and agriculture has been made. All these investments are, by Ethiopian standards, essential elements of modernity. Hence, in many ways, Wollaita is different today than it was four and half decades ago. And yet, the problems of poverty and destitution, unemployment, disease, food insecurity, resource loss- in brief extreme rural hardship and suffering have not only persisted but also increased in magnitude and severity.

The development interventions in the last four and half decades by the government, development partners and others have, by and large, failed to address the key determinants of poverty and destitution, though the failure is greater or lesser in degree depending on the problems and policy interventions concerned. These determinants are, in my view, demographic stress and land shortage, urbanization and commercialization, and livelihood diversification. The issue of drought has also been included, but drought is a common hazard that has affected many parts of the country and is not specific to Wollaita. Because of this failure, the damaging impact of these factors is more pronounced today than before. The study suggests that a considerable policy shift is needed to put these determinants at center stage and to accelerate the pace of development.

I. Introduction

1.1 Objectives of the Study

This study presents a broad review of development interventions in Wollaita undertaken by successive governments, NGOs, and other development partners in the last forty-five years. As conceived by the original sponsors of the study, the purpose was to help initiate a process of deliberation, reflection and debate about the history and impact of development effort in the area. The work was expected to be different from the standard fare widely encountered. It was believed that what was needed was not another data-gathering exercise but a study that would provide deeper insights, knowledge and understanding of the critical problems that peasant farmers in Wollaita are continuing to face despite the considerable effort at economic progress and poverty reduction under different political and economic systems. Sufficient information already exists, and while much of it is not of high quality, it does provide some basic data to allow a work of reflection and critical analysis to be attempted.

More specifically, the work has the following objectives: a) to try to understand why, despite nearly half a century of development effort in which considerable financial, material and human resources were invested in the area, poverty, and all the deprivations associated with it, is still widespread in rural Wollaita; b) to learn from the experiences of the past and to use the knowledge acquired to consider alternative policy options; and c) to engage in a wide ranging public discussion on development issues in Wollaita to enable all stakeholders to get a greater understanding of what must be done to bring about broad-based, pro-poor and sustainable development in the area.

On April 3, 2007, a one-day workshop was held in Wollaita Soddo, to discuss the findings of the study and to consider the policy recommendations that are provided in it. The workshop was jointly organized by Action for Development (AFD) and the Wollaita Development Association (WDA). Among the important issues that were raised for discussion were the economic impact of the political systems established by the three successive regimes in the period under review, and the complex cultural traditions of the people and their development implications. Both subjects are immensely important but have not been seriously considered in the study because they were outside the scope of work provided to the author. It was suggested that WDA should sponsor extended research on these and other important subjects not covered in the present work.

This study is, therefore, by no means definitive. As noted earlier, there are some important subjects that have not been covered. Nevertheless, we believe it is sufficient to initiate debate and reflection by all those who have the welfare of Wollaita peasants at heart.

1.2 Focus of the Study

The author has had many years of experience doing field work in Wollaita, and has produced several studies on various aspects of rural development in the area. After reviewing the available documentation, it was thought best to frame the study around what he believed are key issues that have had a determinant impact on rural livelihoods and poverty in the last four and half decades. This would make the study more focused and less of a general historical narrative. The key determinants are ***demographic stress and land shortage, urbanization and commercialization***, and ***livelihood diversification.*** These are determinants that are of specific relevance to Wollaita. The issue of drought and environmental stress has been raised by a large number of informants interviewed for this study, and while we shall examine the response to it at the conclusion of this report, we recognize that natural hazards are common to most rural producers in the rest of the country and not specific to Wollaita alone.

The work will assess the development interventions of the last four decades in the context of these determinants and how they have impacted on poverty on the one hand, and, on the other, how the development programs pursued in this period have addressed the problems associated with each one of them. Running through the analysis will be the central problem of poverty and destitution and how it has shaped peasant responses and livelihood strategies.

Wollaita is one of the most thickly settled areas of the country, and in some places, the population density compares with that found in the overpopulated areas of south-east Asia. The complex impact of demographic pressure on natural resources and living space, poverty and income, farming systems, the ecological balance of the rural areas, and public health is quite obvious but has not been seriously examined. Wollaita is a land of micro-holdings. As a result of population dynamics, and in part due to historical factors, per capita land holdings have always been small relative to other parts of the country. The evidence indicates, however, that family holdings have been growing smaller through the decades, and in recent years this has been compounded by growing landlessness, especially among the young. It is obvious that *population pressure and land shortage are two sides of the same coin.*

The second factor in our analysis is urbanization and commercialization. Wollaita is one of the least urbanized areas of the country, even by Ethiopian standards. The 1994 census put the total population at 1.17 million with an urban population of nearly seven percent. The comparable national urban population was nearly 14 percent. The estimate in 2005 is 1.68 million, with an urban population of nearly 8 percent; the comparable national urban population at this time is put at 16 percent. The expansion of urbanization is a critical factor for economic growth, agricultural commercialization, employment and poverty reduction.

Finally, the issue of livelihood diversification is significant for our purposes. In conditions of smallholder agriculture such as we have here, diversification has a positive impact on the reduction of rural poverty. A wide variety of opportunities for supplementary income, such as off-farm employment, local based small-scale industry, especially relying on agro-processing, employment through large scale infrastructural and construction schemes are what promote greater diversification

The study was based, apart form available documentation, on the following main sources. In Soddo we had interviews with: key persons, including former civil servants in Wollaita, former employees of WADU, and current government officials; the NGO and business communities; and peasants in three woredas of Wollaita.

Extended interviews in Addis Ababa were conducted with Dejazmach Woldesemayat, former Governor of Wollaita, former staff of WADU, and staff of NGOs engaged (either in the past or at present) in programs inWollaita.

A full list of interviewees used is given in Annex 1.

II. Wollaita: Poverty and Destitution

2.1 Context

The physical and administrative identity of Wollaita has remained unchanged for over a century, except for a brief interlude in the late 1980s and 1990s. Under the imperial regime, the area, then called Wollamo, was an *awraja* within what was then called Sidamo Province. This status continued even after the Revolution, until the Derg undertook the administrative restructuring of the country in the second half of the 1980s. At this point, the name Wollaita disappeared when the seven *woreda*s of the awraja were grouped together with eleven woredas in Gamu and Goffa awrajas to form the North Omo Region. Following the fall of the Derg and the creation of self-governing units within SNNPR, Wollaita was denied the right of local autonomy because its constituent units, the seven woredas (see map in Annex 2), were still part of North Omo Zone. From the second half of the 1990s, citizens of Wollaita waged a long and bitter struggle to reclaim their identity and their language, and to demand the establishment of Wollaita as a Zone with its own local self government. At this time, the government was intent on merging the Wollaita language with three other languages spoken by neighboring ethnic groups into an artificial language called WOGAGODA to be used as the official language of North Omo and in schools and other institutions. After a number of demonstrations and violent protests by citizens and young people in Soddo and other parts of Wollaita, the government finally gave in to the demands of the people, and so, at the end of 2000, Wollaita became a Zone within SNNPR with its own elected Council.

As far back as the early 1960s, Wollaita had seven woredas, but this has now changed. The Zone now contains 12 woredas, an increase of six, which was achieved by a process of internal sub-division. Some of the bigger woredas have been divided into two or three new woredas. Bolosso, for example, has been split into three, Damot Gale into two, and so on. Whether this will facilitate more efficient administration and the delivery of basic services to communities remains to be seen. The process of change was still going on at the time of our field work and for this reason and others, we have kept the old woreda structure in this work

Wollaita is a homogenous society not just in terms of language, culture and shared historical experience, but also in terms of livelihood, and, in large measure, social and economic background. The socio-economic homogenization has been largely a product of deep poverty and destitution. Wollaita is a land of micro-peasants and micro-enterprises, a society poised on a knife edge and subject to frequent crises. Even a cursory look at the agrarian and socio-economic conditions of the area shows a society with deep-rooted structural problems which conventional development strategy, the kind employed in the period under review, has been unable to address. As we shall see in more detail in the pages that follow, the basic characteristics of Wollaita are the following:

> ➢ high population pressure and severe shortage of farm land;

> ➢ poverty and destitution leading to endemic food shortages and periodic pandemics and crop disease;

> ➢ limited urbanization, leading to low employment opportunities and low demand for agricultural products;

> ➤ a low level of rural livelihood diversification, leading to a situation where the "carrying capacity" of agriculture is almost exhausted; and

> ➤ frequent drought affecting large parts of the countryside and depleting the meager assets of farming households.

The land area of Wollaita measures 438,370 hectares, or 4500 km^2, of which 54 percent is currently cultivated, 11 percent employed for grazing, and 21 percent under bush, shrubs and forest cover. In terms of agro-ecology, nearly 60 percent of the land lies in the *woyna-degga*, nine percent in *degga* and 35 percent in the *qolla* zones. More than 75 percent of the human and livestock population are to be found in the first two agro-ecologies which also account for some 80 percent of the food crops produced in Wollaita. The degga and woyna-degga areas produce most of the root crops commonly consumed by the people, as well as teff, wheat, barley, maize, and coffee. On the other hand, maize, sorghum and, at least in the past, cash crops such as tobacco and cotton are the main crops in the qolla areas. The fear of malaria and animal disease, especially trypanosomiasis, was the main deterrent against settlement in the lowland areas, but with progress in the control of the latter disease, the areas are being increasingly settled by hard pressed peasants from the higher altitudes.

The Zone contains some rugged terrain with steep hills and mountains, flat plains and bush and scrub lands. Altitude ranges from 1100 to 3000 meters above sea level. In the woyna-degga areas, where the majority of the people live and where economic activity is concentrated, rainfall is bimodal with the heavy rains from July to September (the *meher* season), and the short rains (or *belg*) from February to April. In normal circumstances, rainfall ranging from 1100 to 1300 mm is expected in the higher altitudes while in the lowlands it may average 600 to 900 mm.

To the best of my knowledge no comprehensive inventory of the resource base of Wollaita (potential and actual) has been made so far. Outside of the crop and livestock sectors there is not much reliable information about the economic resource base that is suitable for development planning and strategic investment. The two basic documents on the socio-economic profile of Wollaita recently prepared by the Department of Finance and Economic Development (2005), and by the Wollaita Development Association, WDA (2003) do not identify any major resources outside these two sectors. In view of the frequency of drought and its devastating impact on people's livelihood, a thorough assessment of the water potential of the Zone would have been necessary but is not available. Wollaita is bordered by the Omo River on the west and there are several other rivers and streams crisscrossing the central and eastern woredas. Damota

Mountain is known to be the source of streams, springs and other water sources for the surrounding area, and yet not much else is known about the water potential of the woredas bordering it. Anecdotal evidence suggests that there is considerable surface as well sub-surface water potential which can be utilized for economic and domestic purposes and yet at present only about 0.4 percent of the land is under irrigation.

On the other hand, there has been over the years a good deal of research on the soils of Wollaita going back to the days of Dejazmach Woldesemayat and WADU. However, some of these studies have shown that due to the nature of the farming system and demographic dynamics, there has been a high degree of environmental degradation, in particular soil nutrient depletion (Eyasu 2000, 2002). The increasing loss of soil fertility has impacted on land management, crop yield and agricultural diversification, thus contributing to greater poverty and food insecurity in the rural areas.

2.2 Population and Demographic Dynamics

We may begin this Section by noting that Wollaita has always been associated with high population. Travelers who passed through the area in the first decade of the twentieth century speak of dense settlements and crowded markets (see Dessalegn 1995). Some were astonished by the high population of the rural areas. There is some evidence that the farming of hillsides may have started in the 1930s, which indicates the growing shortage of land. In the 1950s and early 60s, there was consensus among government officials that the population problem was posing a serious threat to agricultural improvement, and settlement in the lowlands of Wollaita was the solution attempted at the time.

There is broad consensus at present also that population pressure is a critical problem. All the NGO staff and former government officials interviewed for this study identified high population and shortage of land resources, which in most cases were seen as two sides of the same coin, as being the primary causes of growing poverty and food insecurity. Peasant informants were also acutely aware that demographic factors have contributed greatly to existing problems in the area.

Let us examine the basic demographic characteristics of Wollaita at present. To begin with, the population is overwhelmingly rural. According to the 1994 census, Wollaita had a total population of 1.13 million with the urban population making up 6.9 percent. In comparison, the urban population at the national level was 14 percent. The population projection for 2005 shows a total population of 1.7 million with the urban population increasing to 8.7 percent (Tables 1 and 2).

At the country level, the urban population is projected to grow to 16 percent by 2005. Compared with other Zones within SNNPR, Wollaita stands as the least urbanized.

Table 1. Wollaita population by woreda (2005)

Woreda	Rural pop.	Urban pop.	Total
Bolosso	333,145	30,846	363,991
Damot Gale	293,145	33,948	327,093
Damot Woyde	210,513	6,570	217,083
Humbo	135,386	4,851	140,237
Kindo Koysha	197,699	6,396	204,095
Offa	156,521	5,065	161,586
Soddo Zuria	233,427	62,049	295,476
Total	**1,559,836**	**149,725 (8.7%)**	**1,709,561**

SOURCE: DFED 2005.

Table 2. Wollaita population estimates & census (various years)

Source	Year	Rural	Urban	Total
CSO	1966	591,800	8,200	600,000
WADU	1976	?	?	900,000
Census	1984	929,919	40,010	969,929
Census	1994	1,055,156	77,976	1,133,132
Projection	2005	1,559,836	149,725	1,709,561

SOURCE: CSO 1966; WADU 1976; 1984 & 1994 Census; DFED 2005.

Until the latter part of the 1970s, Soddo was the only urban area in Wollaita. Today, Areka and Boditi qualify as urban settlements, though very small in size. Soddo had a population of 8,200 at the time of the 1966 CSO population count. It had grown to 24,600 by the time of the 1984 census, and to over 35,000 by the 1994 census. In other words, the population of Soddo had tripled in this period, though we must bear in mind that urban growth started from a very low base. Much of this growth may be attributed to migration from the surrounding rural areas as well as from other parts of the country on the one hand, and to natural growth, on the other.

Due to the absence of accurate population figures over time, it is difficult to generalize about the growth of the population over the decades. Anecdotal evidence suggests that the growth rate has been very high. The last census uses a growth rate of 2.9. If the 1966 CSO population count is taken as accurate, then we can say that the population of Wollaita has doubled in the space of 30 years. Currently, the area's fertility rate is considered to be one of the highest in the country: the average rural woman here has 6.9 children during her reproductive years. In contrast, productive resources and environmental assets (land, soil, natural vegetation, water resources, etc) have dwindled considerably over the last four decades.

The second characteristic that is important for our purposes is the concentration of the population. More than half the arable land in the Zone is located in the woyna-degga altitude and that is where the concentration of the population is to be found. Bolosso has a population density of 637 persons per km^2, Damot Gale 750 km^2, Soddo Zuria 438 km^2, and for the Zone as a whole the density is 360 km^2. (BFED 2005). Under the circumstances, such demographic concentrations pose grave risks for human health, and are the basis of rural vulnerability and poverty. For comparative purposes, we should note that the population density in SNNPR is 118, in Amhara 108, and Oromia 67 km^2.

A third significant element is that high population has led to immense pressure on environmental resources. Much of the forest cover of the area has long disappeared; there is continuous cropping of farm land. Soil fertility is declining and there is a high rate of soil erosion (Eyasu 2000, 2002). Grazing areas are also declining since all available land, including grazing and marginal land, is being turned into farmland. Farming of steep hillsides, a practice that has expanded since the last four decades, is posing serious environmental consequences.

A fourth element is the great immobility of the population, by which I mean the limited movement of people within the rural areas as well as between the rural and urban areas. The indicators for this are the low urbanization we noted earlier, and the limited history of *long-term or permanent* out-migration that is characteristic of the population. True, Wollaita peasants are known to have traveled to the lower Awash valley and other distant areas in search of jobs, but this has often been short-term migration with the migrants returning home once they have saved enough money. Population immobility is further aggravated by the absence of alternative sources of employment, and by inheritance systems. *Partible* inheritance, that is, the division of the family property among several heirs, in particular, *pre-mortem* inheritance (the transfer of the family property during the lifetime of the parents), which is common in the *enset* zone including Wollaita, tends to discourage young males from leaving the rural areas for an extended period of time. Under this system, male children are reluctant to move out because of the knowledge that they will succeed to the property of their parents however small it may be. Female children, on the other hand, will stay only because they have no other alternative (for more details, see Dessalegn 1995).

The net effect of the demographic stress that is so characteristic of Wollaita is what I wish to call the *saturation of rural space*; this has the following consequences:

➢ Demographic stress has led to the extension of the cultivated area through the utilization of marginal and fragile ecosystems with damaging environmental and economic consequences. This extension has been going on since the 1940s, if not earlier, as the demand for farm land has become increasingly acute. There is a downward movement of the farm population, from the highlands to the lowlands in search of land.

➢ Demographic stress has forced farm households to switch to permanent cultivation. The shortening of fallow or its abandonment altogether, which is now common, has damaged customary farming practices which were sound and sustainable in the past.

➢ Demographic stress has been accompanied by the greater subdivision of the land, giving rise to what I have called micro-holdings and micro-agriculture. As farm plots have become smaller, peasants have shifted to using hand tools instead of the ox-drawn plough, since oxen have become too costly and unaffordable.

➢ Demographic stress has exacerbated environmental stress. The land is now poorer, less productive, and less "healthy". There is widespread erosion, nutrient depletion and loss of water resources. The recurrent environmental shocks since the 1980s –drought, crop and livestock disease, etc.– must be seen in the light of this.

It is clear from the foregoing that the threat of a Malthusian tragedy hangs over Wollaita, though in the last decade or so emergency relief and safety net programs have managed to contain the tragedy from occurring full-scale. The saturation of rural space is a dynamic process, and its repercussions extend to other aspects of peasant livelihood as we shall see later in this Chapter.

2.3 Economic Activities

2.3.1 Land Resources and the Farming System

Land Holding

As was noted in passing earlier, Wollaita is a land of micro-holdings and micro-farming. I make a distinction between small-holder and micro-farming systems. The shift from small-holder agriculture to micro-agriculture may have occurred here in the 1960s: there is no clear consensus on this, but it has definitely occurred. This is a significant shift accompanying the growth of poverty and the stagnation of the rural economy. The shift has been driven in large measure by population growth and demographic stress; shortage of land and the continual subdivision of the land available; environmental deterioration and the loss of soil fertility; lack of employment opportunities and of livelihood diversification; and the land system in place since the second half of the 1970s but whose origins must be sought in the Imperial period.

What is the distinction between micro- and small-holder systems? Micro-farm systems are those in which a household's basic farm assets (oxen, land, labor, livestock) have become insufficient, and peasants become trapped in production for sheer survival. Such systems cannot support the basic subsistence needs of the family, cannot create assets or reserves, and are highly fragile. They tend to easily collapse under even minimum pressure, such as for example a mild drought, limited rainfall variability, or moderate market fluctuation. In the conditions of Wollaita, anyone operating less than 0.5 ha of land is a micro-holder. Small-holder systems, in contrast, are relatively more resilient than micro-systems. While production for basic subsistence is an important element of small-holder agriculture, households have enough assets to produce some surplus and to create more assets. Precise measures of the relative strength of each system are not currently available, but it is evident that a considerable proportion of rural households in the Zone are now engaged in micro-farming.

The land system existing at the time of the Imperial period, before the radical reforms of the Derg, was quite complex, containing different rights to land and different holding arrangements. The three main tenures of the system were tenancy, ownership rights, and a mixture of tenants and owner operators. Land owners came in many different forms, from small owner operators, to local gentry and large landlords. The latter two rented out their holding to tenants. According to a WADU study undertaken in Bolosso in 1971, 23 percent of rural households were tenants, 12 percent were owner-tenants and 65 percent land owners. Average holding for tenants was 0.7 ha. (WADU 1976). This is probably true of other woyna-degga woredas of Wollaita. The radical reform of the Derg in the mid-1970s was to do away with this system and create instead a uniform tenure arrangement in which landlordism was abolished and each farming household had use rights to a plot of land in its kebelle or Peasant Association.

We lack reliable evidence to show how land holdings have evolved in the last four decades, but one can safely argue taking into account population growth and environmental degradation that land sub-divisions have become a standard practice and holdings have grown smaller over the period since the 1960s, if not earlier. Land in Wollaita continues to be an extremely scare asset. In a survey I conducted for an earlier study in two service cooperatives in Bolosso in 1989, I found that 45 percent of the households in my sample held land measuring less than 0.5 ha.; about half of these holdings were 0.25 ha and less. Moreover, 67 percent of households held land below 1.00 ha, and 28 percent between 1.00 and 2.00 ha.. Those considered large owners, holding between 2.00 to 3.00 ha constituted only 5 percent of my sample (Dessalegn 1992). In contrast, the WADU study noted above shows that 49 percent of land owners in Bolosso held land measuring less than 1.00 ha, and 30 percent between 1.00 and 2.00 ha.

The picture at present is comparatively worse. Various documents indicate that two-thirds of the households are micro holders, their holdings measuring less than 0.5 ha. DFED's document noted above shows that average holdings for the Zone is about 0.67 ha, while WDA gives a figure of 0.9 ha, which may be a bit on the high side. Farm households in the lowlands hold slightly bigger plots than those in the higher altitudes due to the low density of the population there. The following data is from CSA's agricultural survey for the *meher* season of 2003.

Table 3.   Distribution of land holdings (%)

Land size (ha)	Households (%)
Less than 0.1	6.0
0.1 - 0.5	47.3
0.51 – 1.00	27.0
1.01 – 2.00	15.3
Above 2	4.4

SOURCE: CSA 2003.

The data indicates that 53 percent of farm households hold land measuring 0.5 ha and less, but unfortunately we do not know much about the distribution of holders in this category. Other evidence suggests that the majority, perhaps about 65 percent of households in this category, hold 0.25 ha or less.

There is also no available information on landlessness and the characteristics of the households in this situation. Landlessness is in fact a serious problem affecting in the main young households. The landless do not appear in the *kebelle* tax registers since they do not pay land taxes. While accurate information may not be available it is evident that the number of landless households is not insignificant. Those in the Table that hold less than 0.1 ha of land are in effect landless since such miniscule plots can hardly provide sustenance to households. In fact, one can argue that anyone in the *enset* farming system with less than 0.15 ha of land is as good as landless. In the light of this, we may estimate the landless population to be somewhere in the neighborhood of 15 percent. Many landless persons survive either as agricultural laborers, or through *kotta* or sharecropping arrangements. *Kotta* is quite widespread in Wollaita and both the poor and the better-off engage in it. According to my Bolosso study noted above, about 37 percent of the sampled respondents were involved in kotta arrangements with neighbors, friends or relatives.

I have argued elsewhere that an average household of up to six members in Bolosso requires 3.3 - 4.8 ha of land to be able to produce enough food and income to sustain the family for a year using customary cultivation practices (Dessalegn 1995). The following Table is based on WADU estimates of field trials in the 1980s.

Table 4. Land sufficiency for different crops in Bolosso (1989)

Crops	Land (in ha.)
Teff/wheat/barley	1,6 – 2.0
Maize/sorghum	1.2 – 1.8
Enset	0.06 – 0.2
Sweet potato/other tubers	0.4 – 0.8
Total	**3.3 – 4.8**

SOURCE: Dessalegn 1995.

The figure for enset is based on wider plant spacing than is currently practiced in the woreda. On this estimate, less than five percent of the households in Wollaita hold enough land to feed themselves all year round.

Farming System

Wollaita is part of what is known as the enset farming system (also called enset complex or enset culture).This system involves the dynamic integration of enset and other root crops (taro, sweet potato, other tubers) with cereal crops in a regime of intensive cultivation. Here enset is a strategic crop determining what cereals to cultivate and how much of the family's land to devote to other crops. Thus, cropping plans, land and labor use, and consumption and marketing decisions depend on the cultivation of enset, the staple food. Moreover, enset and tuber cultivation uses less land than cereal agriculture to cover a family's needs. If the household has sufficient enset established, it will plant crops which have high market value, such as teff, barley, maize and pulses. It is the number of enset planted and their stage of maturation that will determine a household's decision on crop diversification and crop mix. However, enset plants mature anywhere between four to six years depending on the varieties planted and agronomic, ecological and other factors. Thus a farmer in the enset complex has to be quite skilled in long term planning.

The enset farming system has been, until recently, a resilient system. Enset itself can tolerate a considerable degree of moisture loss. Moreover, it can, if hunger is looming, be harvested before it is fully mature. The plant's main enemies are disease and rodents. A farmer in the enset system requires less land than his counterpart in the cereal zone to harvest enough food for the family's needs. The mixture of tubers and cereals also gives families a better chance for survival in the face of environmental shocks. For this and other reasons, the enset system has escaped, until the mid-1980s, the frequent occurrence of famine and food crises that is characteristic of the famine-prone areas of the north and east of the country.

The typical household here divides its plots into three or four fields depending on location and ecological setting. Around the house is the enset garden; beyond that is the *darkua* plot which may grow coffee, enset and tubers such as taro, sweet potato and frequently maize. The outer plot is called the *shoqa* field where maize and other cereals are grown. Some households have a small patch surrounding the *shoqa* which is called *outa* and which is covered with grass and trees. All homesteads have a front yard which is used for threshing and also for cultural purposes. The fields closer to the homestead benefit by organic fertilizer, mainly manure and compost and are more carefully tended than the outer fields. There is now evidence that due to a variety of factors, including soil nutrient depletion, peasants are expanding the *darkua* fields and putting most of their attention on them (Eyasu 2000, 2002). This means peasants are concentrating more and more on enset and tuber crops at the expense of cereals which are grown as cash crops (see also Carswell et al 2000,). In the past, the demand for more food and farm products was met by greater intensification of cultivation. Farmers could produce more by intense cultivation of small plots. At present, the impact of demographic stress and land shortage has forced peasants to shift towards a farming regime using damaging agronomic practices.

Eyasu has argued that in the last two decades or so, cereal crop yield has continued to decline and food insecurity has become a severe problem. He notes that nutrient depletion has occurred in the *shoqa* fields, which account for the largest proportion of arable land in Wollaita where most of the cereal crops are produced.

Moreover it has been shown that peasants have either shortened or abandoned fallowing altogether due to shortage of land and its greater sub-division. While in some communities, some plots are rested for a few months, the common practice currently is for the land to be continuously farmed, thus impoverishing it in the process. The rotational system of cropping widely practiced currently is geared more to securing a family's food needs rather than improving soil fertility. Common rotational approaches are: tuber – maize –tuber – maize; maize – tuber – teff; and sometime teff – maize – pulse – teff (see Carswell). Thus, what we are witnessing is a gradual shift in land management, cropping strategy and land use brought about by the growing vulnerability of Wollaita agriculture. This shift is not a healthy one, and will instead force peasant farmers to continue to damaging the land and to retreat into dependence on root crop for nutrition and household needs.

The present government has placed high hopes on modern inputs, particularly chemical fertilizers to boost productivity and to secure food security. One of the main pillars of the package approach currently employed is greater popularization of fertilizers. In the 1970s, WADU was also keen in promoting agro-chemicals. Table 5 below gives a comparative picture of fertilizer distribution to peasant farmers in the WADU period and the last five years. As can be seen from the Table, fertilizer consumption has not reached the levels attained through WADU's efforts in the 1970s. But even then, it was the more well-to-do peasants who purchased fertilizer; the poor could not afford it even at prices which were low by present standards and partly subsidized. At present, fertilizer prices are very high, peasants are poorer and the farm household has increased in number substantially. Despite the concerted effort to promote greater use of fertilizers since the second half of the 1990s, peasants in Wollaita have been deterred by the high price. Moreover, since a great majority of them are micro-holders, using fertilizer is not very profitable.

Table 5. Fertilizer distributed in the 1970s and 2000s (in quintals)

Year	Fertilizer distributed
1974/75	15,653
1975/76	31,563
1976/77	43,545
1977/78	26,930
1978/79	32,494
1979/80	21,933
2002	15,227
2003	19,690
2004	40,130
2005	22,143
2006	16,672

SOURCE: WADU 1982; DARD files, (Soddo) 2006.

Moreover, the most important means of production, farm oxen, are in short supply in the Zone as a whole. Oxen have been very unevenly distributed as far back as the 1960s. According to a WADU study of 1976, 58 percent of peasant farmers used oxen for cultivation and 42 percent used hand tools only (WADU 1976). Current estimates are that 56 percent of peasant farmers do not have draught power, 25 percent are one-ox households, and only 19 percent own a pair of oxen. In the conditions of micro-holdings, oxen as well as other cattle are too costly to keep. Many of the poor depend either on *kotta* arrangements or schemes involving joint use of the animals.

As noted above, the enset farming system depends on high use of organic fertilizer, especially manure, to maintain soil fertility. This means livestock, particularly, cattle are important assets. A family with sufficient cattle will have enough manure for its fields. However, large numbers of families do not have sufficient livestock and hence not enough manure for their farms. The evidence obtained from the Zone shows that over a third of households do not own any cattle at all, and another 40 percent own only one or two heads of cattle. Poor households depend on traditional schemes of co-rearing or share-rearing of livestock, but even this is becoming difficult because the ranks of the richer households who are the source of the cattle "leased" to the poor are diminishing.

Let us now turn to the subject of productivity and examine the available evidence. Unfortunately, the evidence is not complete as no reliable information is available showing changes in productivity over time. But let us look at the data that is presently at hand. In the 1970s, WADU published crop yield figures for the main cereals it was encouraging peasants to cultivate with greater effort, i.e., teff and maize. Table 6 shows average crop yield figures on peasant farms for both crops for several years; the last column shows best yield figures for these crops in 2004. I have also included a yield estimate made in 1967 by a FAO expert who visited Wollaita at the time.

Table 6. Average Yield of Teff and Maize in Wollaita (1967, 1970s and 2004) (qn/ha)

Year	Teff	Maize
1967	7.00	11.00
1973/74	8.0	20.0
1974/75	6.5	25.3
1975/76	5.4	21.7
1976/77	5.6	20.7
1977/78	4.9	19.2
2004	6.1	20.7

SOURCE: Elton 1967; WADU 1979; DFED 2005.

In the 2004 farming season, the best teff yield came from Humbo woreda, and the best maize yield from Offa. We must stress that the WADU figures are average yield figures for the awraja as a whole and not the best figures achieved in each of those years. Crop yield figures provided by WDA are lower than these: it gives 5 and 15 qn/ha for teff and maize, respectively (WDA 2003). For comparison, my survey of two service cooperatives in Bolosso in 1989, noted above, shows average yield for farmers in both locations was 5 – 8 qn/ha for teff, and 12 – 18 qn/ha for maize.

While the data is certainly not complete, it does indicate the condition of peasant agriculture at present. What the evidence shows is that there has been agricultural stagnation going back at least to the second half of the 1970s. What we see here is rural society caught in the twin scissors of high population growth, and thus more mouths to feed on the one hand, and productive decline and hence less food available on the other.

The foregoing discussion is sufficient to show that under present conditions agriculture in Wollaita has exhausted its potential and is becoming increasingly unviable for the great majority of peasants. In an earlier work on the enset farming system in Wollaita published in 1995, I argued that agriculture here has entered a period of terminal decline and is now facing a long term crisis. The reasons I gave were demographic stress, resource shortage, and agronomic practices which in the past were sound and helped the system to be resilient but are now the cause of its vulnerability. Agricultural intensification, the primary response of peasants to resource scarcity and population pressure, has now failed to deliver the same results and adapt to the immense population expansion of the farm population. While in the past, population growth may have stimulated change and improvements in agronomic practice, demographic stress today has become a serious handicap. In the absence of significant urbanization and out-migration, population increase will lead to productive stagnation and decline. In brief, peasant agriculture is in urgent need of sound and long-term solutions which will bring about the transformation of the enset farming system leading towards something new and more dynamic.

2.3.2 Livelihood Diversification

Livelihood diversification is an important subject in view of the conditions prevailing in Wollaita, but it has not been given the attention it deserves either by government or its development partners. In view of the problem of agricultural stagnation discussed previously, alternative options for employment and income for the rural population are desperately needed. High population growth, micro-holdings, and increasing landlessness means there is an acute demand for non-agricultural employment especially by the young and newly established households. On the other hand, diversification of livelihoods is closely linked to urbanization: greater urban growth will open up opportunities for non-farm employment as well as, of course, greater demand for farm products.

At present, non- or off-farm employment opportunities are extremely limited. The most common form of earning supplementary income for peasants has been and continues to be petty trading. Almost all households in the rural areas are involved in petty trade, frequently itinerant trading. Women are active traders, and most are also involved in selling home-made food and traditional beverages. The plethora of weekly markets as well as small, daily neighborhood markets that are common in rural Wollaita encourages petty trading both for men and women. Wealthier peasants are larger traders since they own pack animals and can transport more goods from one market to another, and can reach more distant markets. Poorer peasants engage in selling and buying small items and do not travel much too far. Women traders are more restricted in their movement than their men-folk. For most peasants, the income that is gained from petty trading is quite small and one sometimes wonders whether the activity has a social more than an economic significance.

Another source of supplementary income for some households is wage labor either on the farms of wealthier households in the locality, or on large, modern farms and agro-industries in distant locations. Employment found in the locality often means working in the peak farm season on land preparation, weeding, harvesting or threshing. Payment could be in the form of cash or in kind. The advantage of this form of employment is that the laborer is not far from his residence and can work on his land (if he has any) in his free time, but such work earns less income.

Wage labor in distant areas was common in the period before the Revolution, when large numbers of Wollaita peasants traveled to the upper and middle Awash Valley to work in the agro-industries and mechanized farms located there. Some even went as far as Wollo to find employment. The mechanized farms in the Rift Valley, in the Awassa area, around the Bilate River and close to Arba Minch, also provided seasonal employment to a good number of Wollaita peasants. During the Derg period, many of these enterprises were nationalized, and peasants were forced to work on them as a matter of government policy. For several months every year, a quota of Wollaita farmers were sent to work on State Farms in the Bilate and Arba Minch areas as well as the Awash Valley practically without payment. This was abolished with the change of government, but many of the State Farms were disbanded. At present, wage labor is available on large farms and agro-industries in the Rift Valley areas, including the Arba Minch area, and in the Awash Valley. In the labor season, young laborers are recruited often by agents of the employing enterprises on market days and in busy urban centers and transported to the work sites. The pay is relatively better, and in more recent years, the working conditions have improved. Income from such employment provides the difference between food for the hungry months and starvation (see Carswell 2000, and Bush 2002, for details).

A new initiative that is being promoted in recent years and which is expected to provide opportunities for supplementary income is micro-finance. There are two main micro-finance institutions in Wollaita, one set up by the governing party in the Region (Omo Micro-Finance), the other through the support of an NGO, World Vision (Wisdom Microfinance). These two institutions provide credit and saving opportunities to their clients, mostly from the rural areas. The first, which is the larger of the two, has been active since 1997, and the second since 1999. The combined beneficiaries of both so far are not more than 15 thousand. While this is a good beginning, it is of course far too inadequate to meet the available need. The institutions lend money to those who wish to invest in some income generating activity; they also provide services that encourage members to save. In addition to these, there are small savings and credit cooperatives established by a number of NGOs which provide similar services. These are operated and managed by peasants themselves.

One form of "employment" for the young in the past (both the Imperial and Derg period) was voluntary recruitment into the army. During the Derg, Wollaita contributed a disproportionately high number of young men to the armed services. Figures are not available but the magnitude could be in the thousands. While many were pressed into service especially in the last years of the Derg when the civil war in the country escalated significantly, some were volunteers who frequently became trained officers. When the Derg army collapsed, most of these soldiers returned to Wollaita, many still carrying their weapons, having been promised land and rehabilitation in their home areas by the new authorities. There were attempts to accommodate some of them by giving them small plots, but there was no land available to distribute to most. Few of the returnees were able to support themselves, and some of them turned to petty crime for survival.

To sum up: There is an immense need for livelihood diversification in Wollaita, but the opportunities currently available are far too limited and highly inadequate. The new initiatives to address the problem, through micro-finance and savings and credit institutions, have only scratched the surface. The urban centers are not providing any opportunities to the rural people; they themselves contain a high level of unemployment. As the rural population becomes poorer, the need for non-farm employment becomes more important and more urgent.

2.4 Vulnerable Livelihoods

2.4.1 Poverty and Destitution

There is broad consensus that peasants in Wollaita are one of the poorest in the country. We have seen in the two Sections above the demographic and asset base of peasant poverty. The standard approach employed in recent studies on poverty in Wollaita is to examine the different faces of poverty by showing social differentiation in rural communities as a whole or within the poor themselves. The argument here is that one needs to design a differentiated approach either to food security (Dagnew 1995), or poverty reduction (Bush 2002). Others note that differentiation among the rural population provides a better understanding of livelihood dynamics (Carswell 2000). For some, the exercise is wealth ranking (based on asset ownership), for others social differentiation, which is more than wealth ranking. The common practice is to divide rural society into three or four wealth or social groups: the rich, the middle, the poor and the absolute poor. This may very well be a useful exercise but for our purposes, it may be more useful to talk in terms of the poor and the destitute.

As I have tried to show above, the great majority of peasants are dirt poor. There are probably not more than 10 percent of rural households which may be regarded as well-off by Regional and national standards. By the standards of rural societies in West Africa, even this small group will be considered poor. In the Wollaita context, therefore, it may be best to make the distinction between the poor and the destitute. What, it may be asked, is the distinction between the two?

The distinction between poverty and destitution and the boundary between one and the other is difficult to determine with any degree of precision; nevertheless, it is a valid distinction to make and is frequently employed by peasants themselves who use a range of criteria and vocabulary to distinguish between those who are poor and those who are destitute. Some of the criteria for determining poverty or destitution commonly employed in rural communities include the following: a) Live assets: these consist of farm oxen, other livestock, and household labor; b) Property, which often means agricultural land, though it may include housing or property in nearby towns; c) Cash income derived either from on-farm or off-farm activities, as well as remittances; d) A combination of any or all of the above. In each particular case, there is a commonly agreed cut-off point which separates one category of peasants (the destitute) from another (the non-destitute). Such measures may present difficulties to those who may wish to construct statistical aggregates or a numerical picture of destitution because the cut-off points may appear to be arbitrarily determined, or vary from one community to another. Thus if in one community a destitute is one who has only one sheep or goat, in another he/she may be defined as someone who owns no livestock at all. Despite this drawback, peasant measurements of destitution are empirically sound because they are based on what communities consider critical assets for rural livelihood. The approach taken by government documents to define poverty on the basis of a minimum level of consumption goods is not radically different from the peasant approach and may be faulted on similar grounds. I have argued elsewhere that since the land reform of the 1970s, live assets, in particular farm oxen and labor power, are the most appropriate factors determining well-being or deprivation among rural households. Poverty and destitution are both states of *livelihood deprivation,* but differing in degree. Both involve the erosion of a household's productive, purchasing and bargaining power on the one hand, and its social and institutional resources on the other. Destitution is an extreme form of deprivation. In this definition, poverty or destitution is seen both as a condition as well as a relationship, an end result as well as a process. In most cases, destitution is a downward slide from poverty, i.e., the destitute are those who were once poor but now find themselves in conditions of extreme deprivation due to the further erosion of their livelihood capabilities and resources.

All the evidence suggests that destitution has been increasing in Wollaita in the last two decades, and the dynamic nature of the problem has important implications. My estimation is that about a quarter of the rural population can be considered destitute and a third may be classed as poor. The destitute are asset-less (no land or miniscule holdings; no oxen; no livestock), unable to feed themselves, wholly or in great part dependent on others or public assistance programs or programs run by the voluntary sector. They are always on the brink of starvation, are subject to health hazards, and easy victims of minor environmental or economic shocks.

It is interesting that individuals and groups from a wide diversity of backgrounds interviewed for this study, including peasants, identified more or less the same cluster of factors as being responsible for growing poverty and destitution in Wollaita. All informants were asked to name three determinants of deprivation that they considered the most critical. The three main causes of poverty frequently cited by former and present government officials and NGO staff were: population pressure, land shortage, and drought and environmental shocks. The opinion of peasants in the focus group discussions we conducted were: land shortage, population pressure, and soil fertility decline. It was quite clear during the discussions we had with all groups that population pressure and land shortage were seen as two sides of the same coin. In most cases, the two were taken as "twins" in which one had a direct impact on the other. Growth in population reduced the available land and other environmental resources in a dynamic spiral. Peasants were clearly aware of the demographic changes in their community and the damaging impact it had on land resources and, equally important, on soil fertility and land management practices.

There were also two other factors identified as contributing to poverty and deprivation. Of the two, the one that was cited more frequently was the absence of a strong culture of saving among the peasantry. Many informants thought that peasants, particularly poor ones spend their meager resources without a thought for the next day and are heavily burdened by loans for money spent on non-economical purposes, such as festivals, and cultural and religious occasions. The second factor noted, thought by a smaller number of informants was the lack of alternative employment opportunities in the rural areas (what we have called livelihood diversification earlier).

2.4.2 Famine and Food Insecurity

The first major famine in the recent history of Wollaita occurred in 1984/85. Peasants in Wollaita, along with others in many areas in the north and east of the country, were victims of mass starvation. The immediate cause of the tragedy was severe drought, but the deeper reason was growing vulnerability and the inability of the peasant agriculture to produce sufficient surplus. Since then, the farming system has been severely destabilized because most households were forced to break the cycle of the enset plantation at the time and following the famine; there was heavy loss of the enset plant due to enset disease caused by bacterial wilt.

The 1984/85 famine may be considered a watershed here because prior to this, serious food crises were few and localized, affecting the dry lands of the awraja. In fact, as noted above, the enset farming system had been relatively more resilient than the cereal-based farming system of the famine prone areas in the north and east of the country and the major famines of the 1960s and 1970s which brought hardship and suffering to many peasants in these parts of Ethiopia had passed it by without much consequence. However, as has been noted earlier in this work, the situation since the 1980s has been dramatically reversed. Since then, hunger and food shortages have become a regular feature of peasants in Wollaita, and crisis interventions by government and NGOs have occurred almost every two years or so. The evidence shows the rural population to be increasingly vulnerable, with a growing number of farm households highly dependent on food aid and other public support programs.

Since the mid-1980s, peasants in Wollaita have suffered hunger and food shortages almost continuously. The good years in the two decades have been very few. The following is a schematic view of the years when there was food crisis of one sort or another.

1984/85	Major famine affecting many parts of Wollaita
1987/88	Food shortage due to enset disease, and poor rains
1990/91	Food shortages, crop disease, poor rains
1994/95	Severe food crisis brought on by drought
1998/99	Severe food crisis due to low rainfall, enset and sweet potato disease; high cattle mortality
2000	Severe crisis continued due to same causal factors as 1998/99
2003	Food shortages due to drought and poor harvests; coffee and animal disease

The evidence thus shows that hunger and peasant hardships have occurred in greater frequency than ever before. The lowland areas are obviously more severely affected than the highland areas, and on occasions localized food shortages may occur which may not attract the attention of the Zonal authorities.

Let us look at the problem of food insecurity in greater detail. The first question to ask is: what proportion of rural households are, under normal circumstances, able to feed themselves from their own resources all year round, for half of the year or less? Obviously, there will be variations: people in the qolla areas (except those benefiting from irrigation schemes) are in most cases poorer than those in the higher altitudes. To my knowledge no attempt has been made to estimate the magnitude of poverty from the point of view of food insecurity. I believe that only a small percentage of households- perhaps no more than 10 to 15 percent- are capable of meeting their food needs for a full year under normal circumstances. At the bottom, perhaps one third of the households cannot feed themselves except perhaps for a few months in the year, and anywhere up-to 15 to 20 percent cannot feed themselves at all. The following Table gives the number of people that were dependent on food aid for the last eight years.

Table 7. Wollaita: Population Dependent on Food Aid (1994-2001)

Year	No. of food aid recipients
1994	202,000
1995	236,000
1996	120,000
1997	120,000
1998	--
1999	246,900
2000	358,837
2001	236,800

SOURCE: DARD files (Soddo), 2006.

The government's Productive Safety Net Program was launched in Wollaita in March 2005 and has been operational for slightly over a year. DARD files show that in its first year of operations, the beneficiaries who were set to work in public works programs numbered 263,760. In addition there were 42,704 beneficiaries who were given free assistance because they were unable to work, and 10,890 were supported through what is called the Household Package program. The total figure of dependents for the year was 317,354, making up over 20 percent of the rural population.

Many informants interviewed for this work were of the opinion that peasants have acquired a dependency culture. There is, they maintain, a tendency to look to outside support rather than try to stand on one's own feet. There is a high degree of dependency on food aid, public assistance programs and support from the voluntary sector and also religious institutions. This may very well be the case but, if so, it is a new behavior brought on by unrelenting poverty and extreme hardship.

2.4.3 Pandemics and Congested Living

The rural population of Wollaita has suffered a series of pandemics in the last six to eight decades, and while there may be many factors that are responsible for this tragedy, what I have earlier called the saturation of rural space and the congested form of living that this has given rise to must be included as one of the significant factors. I shall here review briefly some of the main pandemics in the last three to four decades.

As noted above, peasant homesteads are surrounded by rich plant growth, and such plant growth frequently serves as breeding ground for disease vectors such as mosquitoes. The medical history of Wollaita has not been sufficiently investigated, but all the indications we have suggest that the population here has been the victim of wide-spread health crises more frequently than comparable communities outside the *enset* zone. Peasants in Wollaita have been subject to periodic outbreaks of devastating pandemics, of which the main ones in the period between the 1930s and 1990s include small-pox, typhus, malaria, yellow fever, cholera, meningitis, and most recently diarrheal diseases[1].

According to oral informants, serious epidemics of small-pox and typhus hit Bolosso and the adjacent areas killing innumerable people, and forcing some to

---

[1] What follows is based in part on Dessalegn 1995; sources for the discussion are also given there.

flee to the high mountain retreats in the first half of the 1930s. The 1957-58 malaria epidemic, said to be the worst in Africa, affected some three million people in the densely populated areas of the country, mostly in the *woyna degga* and *degga* environments. The epidemic, which public health officials initially mistook for typhus or relapsing fever, quite probably swept through Wollaita though we unfortunately know little of its impact. One of my informants on Wollaita medical history believes that there was a devastating outbreak of what he calls "ye-tinfash beshita" (disease transmitted by breath) which spread through Wollaita and Kambatta in 1957 killing many people; this coincides with the malaria epidemic that Fontaine and others have written about, but we do not know whether the two events are one and the same. The early 1960s saw most of Bolosso and the lower altitudes of the *awraja* devastated by yellow fever, again said to be one of the worst outbreaks of its kind in Africa. The epidemic is said to have traveled up the Omo valley and may have affected over a million people in the country. The most active breeding ground of the mosquito vector was the leaves and stem of *enset* and taro plants, and this explains why much of the *enset* zone was seriously affected. While in the rest of the country the epidemic lasted from 1960 to 1962, it did not work itself out in Wollaita until 1964. The 1970s were also difficult years for the peasantry here because of repeated outbreaks of cholera.

In the late 1980s, coming soon on the heels of the famine, a meningitis epidemic swept through much of Wollaita. The epidemic, which was preceded by a malaria outbreak in the lower altitudes, started in the last quarter of 1988 and was not finally brought under control until the middle of 1989. In early 1989, nearly two-thirds of the rural population, men and women in the 2 to 30 year age bracket, were said to be at risk. The epidemic was mostly confined to the *enset* growing areas of Sidamo, Gamo Goffa and southern Shoa. The attack rate was believed to be 200 per 100,000 population, and while the actual death toll will probably never be known, there is reason to believe that it was very high.

In between these large-scale pandemics were localized outbreaks of disease often attacking children and those suffering from malnutrition. It is known for instance that in 1983 there was a localized outbreak of relapsing fever in central Wollaita, with nearly 700 deaths reported. Furthermore, in the period November 1988 to October 1989, and again in the same period in 1990-91, there were exceptionally high rates of child mortality in the rural areas. According to the evidence, the cause of the disaster on both occasions was probably an outbreak of disease; anthropomorphic measurements taken at the time did not reach below the threshold deemed to indicate severe malnutrition and to require emergency assistance. Mortality figures for each of the two years are shown to be almost twice as high as the national average. Finally, localized and small-scale epidemics of typhus, cholera and malaria are not uncommon in the *awraja*.

In the late 19990s and early 2000s the major health hazards have been diarrheal diseases on the one hand, and HIV/AIDS on the other. Malaria is still an endemic threat, especially in the lowland areas. Diarrheal disease has recently been raging in many parts of the Wollaita countryside but has now been contained. On the other hand, the spread of HIV/AIDS is now a major problem which will worsen the poverty situation and have a damaging impact on development initiatives under way. At present there is no accurate evidence of the magnitude of the problem and how fast the disease is spreading especially in the rural areas. While it was initially confined to the towns, particularly Soddo and Boditi, it is believed to be spreading rapidly among the peasantry (FGA 2006). The available evidence shows that young people, those between 15 to 29 are the most at risk, with more women than men in the urban areas infected. According to FGA, among people voluntarily tested for the disease in Soddo in 2006, nearly seven percent were found to be HIV positive. Among women tested in Soddo health center in 2003, 11 percent were found to carry the disease. The evidence from Zonal officials and NGOs is that the disease is posing a major threat to lives and livelihoods in the rural areas. A good number of NGOs based in Wollaita are engaged in the preventive programs which at present include counseling on safe sex, provision of condoms, and support to families affected by the disease.

The dense settlement that is typical of Wollaita, the lack of proper public health programs, and the shortage of clean water has meant poor personal and environmental hygiene and favorable circumstances for the rapid spread of communicable diseases. The customary practice of keeping livestock in the home at night together with the family, which has health implications, must be seen as a response to the shortage of space on the farm.

III. Development Interventions in Wollaita Since the 1960s

3.1 Government: Development Policies

In this Chapter we shall review in broad terms the development policies and outcomes of the three successive regimes since the 1960s. The aim is to examine their development interventions so as to draw valuable lessons for our purposes. A full and detailed examination of the record of rural development during the last four and half decades will require a voluminous book; thus we have to restrict ourselves to discussing the main principles, frameworks and outcomes in each particular case.

3.1.1 The Imperial Regime

The beginning of modern forms of development in Wollaita may be dated to the early 1960s with the appointment of Dejazmach Woldesemayat as Governor of Wollaita[2] in the wake of the coup attempt to topple Emperor Haile Selassie and his government. One of the instigators of the coup attempt was Germame Neway, who was the Governor of Wollaita in the 1950s. The Dejazmach took up his post in September 1962, and from this time up to 1970, when he was transferred to Awassa as Vice-Governor of Sidamo Province, he initiated and implemented a wide variety of basic development programs whose impact is still visible today. When he handed over his Wollaita governorship and moved to Awassa he left behind him an impressive record of achievement which in many respects has not yet been surpassed. His record is all the more remarkable because it was achieved in a relatively short time and with very limited funds. The Dejazmach gained wide recognition not only in the awraja but among the modern elite in the country at the time for his accomplishments, and he still has a high stature and reputation in Wollaita today.

Dejazmach Woldesemayat

The Dejazmach brought what for the time was a novel approach to development work, established clean and efficient administration, and inspired those working under him but above all the people of Wollaita with his personal commitment and dedication to duty. He was energetic, focused and hard working. He spent most of the day out in field or in project sites rather than in the office. The secret of his success was based on the following four principles:

i) Clean and efficient administration, or, what in today's terminology would be called, good governance. The elimination of corruption, waste and inefficiency, he believed, was important to win public confidence which in turn was a central element in successful development work.

ii) Devotion to duty and personal dedication and initiative on the part of the leadership. Effective leadership and confidence on the part of the people on the leadership is possible only through such means.

---

[2] The rank of Dejazmach was given to the governor in 1972. It was during the Derg in the 1970s that the name of the awraja was changed from Wollamo to Wollaita. In this section I shall continue to refer to the governor as Dejazmach and the awraja as Wollaita for convenience. I had two long interview sessions with the Dejazmach in September and what follows is based on the interview and the documents he kindly provided.

iii) Commitment to development and the well-being of the people at large. The work of government must be to promote the well-being of the people, and development work has to be undertaken even under difficult or unfavorable circumstances.

iv) Effective development work is possible with limited resources. Effective work requires the close participation of the people. The participatory approach reduces the dependence on external (i.e., government or donor) found and resources.

When the Dejazmach arrived in Soddo to take up his post, there was hardly any basic infrastructure or services to speak of in the awraja. There were no telecommunication services, no electricity, and no financial institutions or banks. Such was the condition of the main road from the national to the awraja capital that it took two days to travel from Addis Ababa to Soddo. Communication among the woredas was arduous because of the lack of serviceable roads. There were no health and educational institutions, except one small hospital run by SIM in Soddo, one public school in Soddo (Dej. Beyene), and a clinic and primary school in Dubo managed by the Catholic mission. There were no agricultural services to speak of, and no urban centers except Soddo which was a town of a few thousand people, and Boditi which was even smaller, both with no water supply for the residents. The Dejazmach was thus faced with a daunting task. His first major tasks were three-fold:

i) To improve the basic physical infrastructure of the awraja as rapidly as possible, especially telecommunications, road transport, electric power, and clean water supply for Soddo town to begin with and for other centers later.

ii) To reform the administration of the awraja, in particular his own office, the police and the courts. This was to eliminate corruption and abuse of authority, and promote good governance. In the process of this reorganization, Wollaita was divided into seven woredas, doing away with the existing 5 woredas and 12 sub-woredas.

iii) To establish a development fund through the direct contribution of the people, in cash and in kind, and to mobilize the people to participate in the development of their community.

The last point is important because that was to be the key element in his success. The Dejazmach believed that the people themselves, properly mobilized could undertake considerable development work. The system he set up for this purpose had two elements. The first one was that each person was to contribute a small sum of money (from 50 cents to one Birr) every year towards the development fund. This was to be paid at the time each person came to pay his/her annual taxes. The money was scrupulously managed and used for the purpose for which it was collected. According to the record I had access to, a total of 1.22 million Birr was raised through this means from 1963 to 1970, of which all except 45,797 Birr, i.e., only four percent, was employed to undertake development work. The four percent was used to pay salaries and per diems for essential staff. The second element was that everyone was required to participate in the development work being undertaken by providing labor and other assistance.

The works accomplished under the Dejazmach are too numerous to list here; we shall instead look at some of the major ones for our purposes. In his first year; in office, Wollaita had a telephone service, electricity and banks. The roads linking all the woredas were built soon after, in the process of which a number of bridges, including the bridge over the Omo River, were constructed. Several new towns, including Areka, were planned and built. The rudiments of basic infrastructure were put in place in each woreda. In the second half of his governorship, numerous schools, clinics, and several urban water supply systems were constructed. Agriculture was not neglected, and the Dejazmach made efforts to put in place an extension service and to introduce new varieties of maize and other crops. While limited in scale, he also tried to popularize the use of chemical fertilizer to improve crop yield. The first population count and complete survey of the soils of the awraja were undertaken in 1966. All these programs were accomplished in large measure with the development fund collected from the people, though there was some injection of donor support in the form of technical assistance and expertise.

The Dejazmach is closely associated with the resettlement experience of Wollaita. In his first tour of the awraja upon taking up his post, he was struck by the dense settlement of the rural areas. He was convinced that the solution to the population pressure was resettlement. Resettlement was to be the solution not only for population pressure but also for tenancy. The first settlement he organized was the Abela settlement in the Humbo lowlands. This settlement was initially tried by Germame during his governorship but was abandoned without success. The settlement involved not only land hungry peasants from the Wollaita highlands but also poor peasants from northern Ethiopia. While initially the cooperative form of organization was tried this was soon dropped in favor of private plots for each household measuring five hectares. The crops grown were cotton, tobacco, red pepper, as well as maize. The scheme was quite successful and attracted donor attention. The second settlement was at Bele in Kindo

Koysha, involving mostly Wollaita peasants from the highlands. This was not, relatively speaking, as successful as the Abela settlement but the scheme continued long after the Dejazmach had left his post.

What lessons can we draw from the experiences of the first decade of development in Wollaita and the contribution of Dejazmach Woldesemayat? The governor's accomplishments are the result of a combination of personal commitment and good governance, on the one hand, and popular mobilization and participation on the other. While the conditions were different then from what they are today, the principles on which development work was based are not time-bound and are applicable in present circumstances.

Wollaita Agricultural Development Unit (WADU)

In the 1970s, the principal development actor in the awraja was the Wollamo (later Wollaita) Agriculural Development Unit, WADU, which was financed mainly by the World Bank with a third of the cost covered from contributions by the Ethiopian government. The initial agreement to establish WADU was made during the Dejazmach's tenure of office and as a result of his successful settlement program. At first conceived as a scheme for credit to farmers, it was later transformed into a comprehensive integrated development program. WADU was to have two phases, in the first of which was to cover two woredas and in the second all seven woredas. Formally launched in 1970, it was able to accomplish its first phase objectives in three years and used the remaining five years to cover the whole of the awraja. But unfortunately it was caught in the chaos, upsurge and topsy-turvy of the Revolution and its aftermath. It was closed down in 1984 though it was in effect non-functional after 1982. The total funds utilized by the organization until 1982 is put at 47.9 million Birr, of which the first phase cost 12 million (WADU 1980, 1981; interview with Dessalegn Tanga). The agency had a large staff: at the end of 1979, it had 1000 employees of which high and middle level staff numbered 350.

WADU's main mission was to promote a comprehensive development program in Wollaita, the chief element of which was the improvement of agricultural production through a wide variety of extension and support services. These latter included promoting peasant consumption of modem inputs such as fertilizers, improved seeds, and pesticides through credit programs, the promotion of cooperatives, and training of peasants to use better agricultural practices. Other major elements of the agency's program emphasized land conservation through bund building, gully control and rehabilitation of vulnerable soils; this involved large-scale afforestation. WADU was also to manage the resettlement schemes already established and to improve and expand them. Finally, livestock breeding and protection, and infrastructure building (rural access roads, water development, etc.) were also included. WADU established a number of service centers throughout the woredas it was operating in for delivery of services, and to be used as training centers as well as supply stores.

After the first phase of operations, the most successful by all accounts, when the program had reached more than 20 thousand households, WADU realized that while the potential for improvement in peasant agriculture was considerable the potential for *development* of rural Wollaita society was very limited. The scope for increased family income, and increased employment *outside* agriculture was very limited. High population pressure, and severe land shortage provided little room for rural development in the broad sense of the term. WADU therefore believed that it had to set its sights on limited goals and limited achievements. It consequently sought to actively promote increased production of crops both to improve peasant consumption and family cash income. This was to be achieved not really through improved cultural practices. Peasant agriculture would not be significantly changed, and modernization involving high technology would not be considered. The aim was to apply green technology techniques on a limited basis. WADU also aimed at promoting food security in Wollaita as a development objective. Better consumption would lead to a healthier population. The agency was of the opinion that there was sufficient room to raise agricultural production needed for consumption purposes but that the scope for expansion of cash crop production, and hence raising peasant income, was limited. The main source of cash income was to come from raising cotton, coffee, chilies, and haricot beans, but land shortage was a serious constraint.

WADU's planned development of consumption crops involved expanding production of grain crops and reducing production of enset and other root crops and tubers. The agency felt that improvements in peasant diet would come from greater consumption of cereal crops and reduced consumption of root crops. It wanted to discourage tuber crop production therefore for dietary, health as well as economic reasons. Less tubers grown would release land for grain and cash crop production. Increased income for the family was to come from cash crop production, but the potential for increased income through this means was limited. Its projected plan for the period 1974-1994, with WADU fully operational was that net incremental income per household would rise from 200 to 350 Ethiopian dollars (as the Birr was then called) per year by the end of the plan period. This was based on some heroic assumptions: that there would not be dramatic increases in prices of agricultural inputs and services, and that peasant holdings will not deteriorate in quality or in size. There was also another side to the problem which WADU did not full appreciate. This was that the farming system of Wollaita peasants is an intricate one, and, as was noted by Peter Byrne, the last consultant to evaluate the agency, WADU failed to properly understand the system, thus making its interventions less effective than they would have otherwise been. It would be difficult for a peasant in the enset system, as described above, to abandon tuber cultivation without an assured incentive that would be too good to refuse.

By 1980, more than half the population of Wollaita was participating in WADU programs. In the area of land conservation, road building, promotion of modem inputs, WADU's achievements were considerable. Mainly due to the promotion of fertilizer use, there were also improvements in crop yield. Moreover, it expanded the resettlement program so that by the early years of the 1980s the settler population had grown to over 1800. In terms of its main objectives, however, ie., promoting food security, the results were disappointing. Bolosso and other areas in Wollaita remained food insecure, family income became depressed, and rural poverty did not decline but grew instead. Part of the reason had to do with events that WADU planners did not anticipate, viz., the Revolution, and the damaging rural policies that accompanied it.   .

The failure of WADU was that it was too optimistic and that it underestimated the seriousness of the problems facing rural Wollaita. While peasants here are hard working, industrious and receptive to new ideas, they remain burdened by a rigid farming system which reproduced mini-enterprises. This system originally evolved to meet the problems of land shortage and population pressure, but over the years its disadvantages came to outweigh its advantages. The major elements of the system are miniscule holdings, intensive and continuous cultivation giving rise to soil depletion, and decreasing productivity. WADU did not seriously consider promoting alternative farming systems in Wollaita but limited itself to providing support to farmers to enable them to overcome some of the weaknesses of the system. In his evaluation report, Peter Byrne raises a number of issues and criticisms. He argues that WADU's impact has been considerable and the achievements are increased crop production, reduced livestock mortality, increased coffee production and improvements in soil conservation. Moreover, he notes, the agency has had a strong impact, not quite quantifiable, on increased awareness of the ability of the Wollaita farmer to improve crop and livestock productivity. He is critical of the agency for its lack of adequate research effectiveness, lack of proper understanding of the farming system, poor planning and evaluation of project impact, poor financial management, and high staff turnover. Since adequate data had not been collected, he notes, assessing the economic impact of the agency's programs on farmers is impossible. He goes on to point out that "vast overstaffing of WADU has existed since 1977/78 resulting in over 50% of all Project costs being devoted to staff salaries and administration (Byrne 1981). This is in sharp contrast to Dejazmach Woldesemayat's development approach of using limited funds to accomplish effective work (see above).

To these, we may add a few other challenges. Although WADU succeeded in establishing numerous multi-purpose cooperatives, the organizations were weak and ineffective because of managerial and financial problems. Misappropriation of funds by the cooperative leadership was not infrequent. The lack of supervision, proper training and attention on the part of the Agency were factors for the failure of the organizations. In addition, the credit program was in poor condition due to a high rate of default by participating farmers. According to the evidence, more than 2 million Birr was owed to the Agency by farmers who failed to pay both the principal and interest. This may be due in part to the unsettled conditions of the times brought on by the Revolution.

But, more importantly for our purposes, we need to ask: what has been WADU's record from the point of view of what we have called earlier the key determinants of poverty in Wollaita? The answer in brief is the record is by and large poor. The agency gave inadequate attention to the issue of population growth and the problems raised by demographic stress both on resource access and livelihoods. True, WADU was engaged in the settlement program and settlement has been seen by some as a solution to population pressure. However, the Agency inherited the program from the previous administration. It was the Dejazmach who had established the settlement schemes in both Abela and Belle. The strategy of changing the cropping system pursued by WADU by encouraging a shift from emphasis on root crop cultivation to cereal cultivation was, under the prevailing circumstances, ill advised. The enset farming system is a product of adaptation to high population pressure. The system, with its smaller demand for land, is better suited to provide food security than the cereal-based farming system with its relatively large land requirements. However, the enset system had become caught in a trap because of an inordinate rise in population.

In terms of urbanization and livelihood diversification, the two other key factors of poverty we have identified, WADU's record is inadequate. The Agency virtually neglected the urban areas. The reigning ideology at the time was that development was to come by modernizing rural production, and accordingly, the urban areas were given less emphasis. WADU, being an agricultural development project, was rural oriented and had a modest objective to accomplish as noted above. In contrast, the Dejazmach's strategy in this regard was better: he built several new towns, provided basic infrastructure in them, including clean water supply, communication and power. His attempt to encourage manufacturing enterprises in Soddo was a step in the right direction. In terms of livelihood diversification, the record is slightly better. WADU's attempt to promote improved bee-keeping by using modern hives were encouraging. The cooperatives were given the task of implementing the new technique. WADU also made some attempt to provide training and upgrading of local artisans. Both of these were meant to provide supplementary income to farmers but the success rate was limited.

After 12 years of operations and having spent nearly 48 million Birr, WADU was closed down by the decision of the new military government. WADU's experience holds some good lessons for us all: the task of promoting development in Wollaita is complex but that task must first be based on a clear and in-depth understanding of the lives and livelihoods of the people and the farming systems that they have evolved over the generations.

3.1.2 The Derg and Agricultural Socialism

The Revolution that overthrew Imperial rule in 1974 was received with a good deal of support by the population at large. The first measure of the new authorities, the Derg, was to legislate a radical land reform. While there was a good deal of uncertainty among the peasantry about the events unfolding at the time, the government did win a measure of popularity in the countryside once the significance of the land reform (announced in early 1975) became clear to the peasantry. Most peasants welcomed the dispossession of the landed classes, which was one of the aims of the reform. Soon, however, there was a radical change as the Revolution hardened and adopted Soviet-style socialism as its guiding principle.

The 1975 land reform, comparable to the Chinese and Vietnamese reforms in its thoroughness, transferred all land to *public ownership* and prohibited all forms of private land ownership, including those of smallholders. The peasant household had only usufruct rights over the land it cultivated. It could not transfer those rights to others by sale, lease or mortgage. At one stroke the landed classes were completely dispossessed without compensation. Land redistribution was to proceed on the principle of equalization of holdings, and hired labor was forbidden. In effect, land was nationalized, and the state replaced the landlord as the owner of the land.

Local peasant communities were empowered to set up what were known as Peasant Associations (PAs). These organizations were made up of all household heads in each community and given authority to redistribute land, maintain common assets, resolve conflicts and enable development activities to take place in their areas. They were also used to carry out a variety of political functions, including collecting taxes, maintaining law and order, channeling directives to the peasantry, enforcing the government's grain requisition program and later recruiting young men for the military.

The main flaw of the land reform was that it gave rise to a leveling down of individual holdings as more beneficiaries made claims to land than could be accommodated. Furthermore, both the new tenure and the mandate given to PAs encouraged the practice of periodic redistribution of land to accommodate new claimants and to correct imbalances. In the 1980s, fresh redistribution of land was taking place in several parts of the country, often initiated by extension agents as part of a readjustment plan designed to pave the way for the introduction of collectivization. Redistribution frequently meant losing part of one's allotment or being relocated elsewhere. In brief, reform gave rise to *insecurity of holdings* which was further exacerbated by subsequent policies. It transformed rural Ethiopia into a society of self-laboring peasants.

One positive outcome of land reform, which should be noted in the light of the political changes taking place in the country at present, is that reform struck at the roots of ethnic discontent and the conflict latent in ethnic relations, relations in which the land question was always in the foreground and frequently determined conditions of power and influence. By distributing land to peasants resident in a community (and this was one of the justifications of Peasant Associations), reform dispossessed all landlords, in particular those who were not indigenous to the community concerned. This meant that outsiders, mainly landlords from the northern provinces who had extensive holdings in the southern regions and the minority areas, were expropriated and their property was distributed to the indigenous population.

Throughout most of the 1980s, rural policy consisted of state agriculture, collectivization, grain requisitioning, resettlement, and villagization. Wollaita peasants were involved in all these unpopular programs. Agricultural socialization was launched soon after land reform, with heavy investment in state agriculture first, followed by the push for what were known as peasant producer co-operatives. According to the Ten Year Plan drafted in 1984 and expected to run to 1993, the 'transition to socialist agriculture' was to be largely complete by the end of the plan period, when the socialist sector of rural production was expected to become dominant. By that date the sector was expected to be operating some 60 per cent of the cultivable land of the country; food sufficiency was also to be achieved by then. Planners placed high hopes in particular on producers' co-operatives, which were expected to operate over 50 per cent of the nation's cultivable land (some 3-5 million ha) by the end of the plan period. Co-operatives were believed to be more cost-effective, and were seen as the main engine of rural transformation. By the end of the 1980s, however, socialist enterprises altogether were operating only a small percentage of the arable land of the country.

Numerous producer-cooperatives were established in several parts of Wollaita in the 1980s. Peasants were in large part pressured into joining the cooperatives, and those that were unwilling were evicted from their land. These cooperatives and their counterparts in the rest of the country benefited from government support, despite that, however, they performed poorly, were inefficient and wasteful. Almost all the enterprises in Wollaita employed oxen for cultivation and labor was organized on a 'work gang' basis but the gangs were rarely formed on the basis of compatibility, ability or performance. The system of remuneration, which was modeled on the Chinese point system, was not well received by many peasants here because they believed it encouraged incompetence and waste.

The main state farm in the Wollaita area was the Bilate State Farm, which was in private hands during the Imperial period. The story of state agriculture here as well as in the rest of the country is one of mismanagement, of wasted resources, and financial loss on a large scale. State agriculture was initially cobbled together out of a large number of previously owned mechanized farms, many of which were loss-making and burdened with debt. In the beginning state farms' holdings were small, but less than half a decade later they had expanded fourfold. This feverish expansion, which also involved peasant evictions, turned out later to have been poorly planned, and in some cases environmentally damaging. Some large-scale farm complexes were subsequently abandoned, owing, among other things, to poor planning, mismanagement and/or abusive labor deployment practices.

In brief, agricultural socialization was plagued with inefficiency, waste of resources, mismanagement and poor morale among participants and employees. To the surrounding peasantry, socialized enterprises, particularly co-operatives, were a threat, a burden, or unwelcome competitors for resources. The enterprises were highly favored by the state even though their contribution to the nation's food needs or to state revenue was almost negligible. Co-operatives and state farms alike relied on *corvee* peasant labor in peak seasons: peasants were compelled to work on them during ploughing, weeding and harvesting but were not paid for their work, and on occasions they were expected to meet their own expenses if the work lasted more than a day. Wollaita peasants were taken to the Awash Valley, and sometimes as far away as Wollo to work on state farms.

Another policy that embittered all peasants in Wollaita as well as elsewhere, was grain requisitions. Socialist enterprises had to sell all their surplus produce to state agencies at prices that were pegged very low by the government. Individual peasants in turn had to hand over a predetermined quota of grain to the state purchasing agency, the Agricultural Marketing Corporation (AMC), at similar prices; the grain quota was imposed on all peasants living in so-called surplus producing regions, and this in effect involved about four-fifths of the country's farm households. Many areas in Wollaita were designated as surplus producing. The government distorted the grain market to the great disadvantage of peasant producers by attempting to regulate grain prices and the flow of grain in the country. The justification for grain requisitioning was that it would hold food prices down in the urban areas, and undermine and, in the long run, eliminate private grain marketing. In the end, none of these objectives was achieved: peasants continued to be squeezed by AMC and skinned by grain merchants, while food prices in the urban areas rose steadily all though the period under discussion.

Another program that was seen as eventually part of the socialist transformation of the country was villagization. The objective of the program was to bring dispersed homesteads together in villages so that it would be easy to provide basic services such as health, education, and water supply. From the second half of the 1980s, there was an accelerated effort to build as many villages as possible. By the end of the decade over a quarter of rural households in the country were moved into villages. Villagization was quite unsuitable in heavily populated areas such as Wollaita where there were few vacant lands to build villages. Moreover, peasants here lived in dense settlements which almost resembled villages. Additionally, there were enset and other root crops planted all around the homestead which was meant to provide food for the family for several years. Nevertheless, peasants in Wollaita were moved into villages, and sometimes this meant moving a short distance –perhaps a few meters- from their original homes. Villagization here disrupted cropping plans, and farming strategies leading to considerable loss and hardship for most peasants.

The final major component of the Derg's socialization program was resettlement. Planned settlement during the Derg began in the latter part of the 1970s but became a major undertaking in the 1980s especially after the disastrous famine that occurred in the middle of that decade (for this, see Dessalegn 2003). Resettlement was meant to relieve the population pressure of the vulnerable areas and bring about the environmental rehabilitation of these areas on the one hand, and, on the other, to promote food security. But resettlement also formed part of the Derg's policy of agricultural socialisation. In the period 1984-86, the Derg resettled some 600,000 people mostly in the lowlands of western Ethiopia. In this same period, some 33,000 settlers lost their lives due to disease, hunger, and exhaustion, and thousands of families were broken up. It is estimated that close to half a billion Birr was spent on emergency resettlement, but the cost of the damage caused to the environment, of the loss of livestock and other property, or of the distress and suffering it caused to numerous people and communities will never be known.

There were two types of settlement schemes: "conventional" schemes, which were large-scale and based on collectivization and mechanized agriculture, and "integrated" schemes, which were small-scale and located on land owned by Peasant Associations. The majority of settlers were from Wollo, North Shewa and Tigrai; there was also a sizable population from Kembatta, Wollaita and northern Gojjam. Derg officials were convinced that there was plenty of unused arable land in many parts of the country, especially in the southwest to accommodate large numbers of settlers. In the end, this proved unfounded, and the settlement schemes were undertaken for the most part in dry or semi-dry areas which proved to be unsuitable to ox-plough farming and posed serious health hazards to both highland farmers and their livestock. Moreover, the settlement program was undertaken without the consent of the settlers themselves.

The program involved considerable environmental damage. Large areas were cleared of their vegetation to build homesteads, to acquire farmland and to construct access roads. Resettlement in particular failed to recognize the rights of local people or the carrying capacity of the areas of settlement. It created conflict between the host population and settlers. It also failed to adapt farming practices to the agro-ecological conditions of the lowlands, and as a consequence, the environmental damage involved was quite considerable. Moreover, one of the objectives of resettlement was to reduce the population pressure of the highlands and thereby to control natural resource degradation.

In the end, resettlement had no or limited impact on population pressure or land rehabilitation. On the contrary, it created population pressure and an extensive process of degradation in the host areas. As resettlement was undertaken without the consent of the population involved, the program was unstable from the very beginning. Many settlers abandoned the schemes and returned to their home areas all through the 1980s. The fall of the Derg prompted a large number of settlers to trek back home, although some of them subsequently returned to the settlement schemes of their own free will.

All the Derg's socialization schemes, including villagization and resettlement, were dismantled immediately following the announcement of the Mixed Economy reforms in 1990, on the eve of the Derg's collapse. The reform failed to win the Derg the support of the peasantry. The hard line policies of agricultural socialization had embittered the great majority of rural cultivators who were also exhausted by recurrent famine, food shortages, and the extractive programs of the state. In the case of Wollaita, the Derg failed to address the specific problems that faced peasants here. The land reform did not have any impact on population pressure, resource scarcity and diversification. When resettlement was abandoned, many peasants returned home to demand land for their livelihood.

3.1.3 The Present Government and Agriculture-Led Development

The Federal government's new agricultural policy is based on what is known as rural centred, agricultural-led development strategy or ADLI. The policy document argues that the goal of economic policy is to ensure rapid and sustainable development, and this will be possible only through the prior development of agriculture (FDRE 2001). What 'rural-centred development' involves, and why it was chosen over other alternatives is not clearly spelt out, but the strategy emphasizes that small-holder agriculture will be given high priority, a welcome change from the rural policies of the later Imperial period and the Derg. The focus of development activity will thus be agriculture, the justification being that without a rapid rate of agricultural growth the progress of the other sectors of the economy will be slowed down. Agricultural growth is also seen as a guarantee against food insecurity. Peasant agriculture is envisaged to be the basis of the expected rapid growth, though private commercial investors are encouraged to play a "supportive role".

Rapid agricultural growth, it is argued, will not only improve the living standards of the farming population but will also benefit urban residents by offering them access to cheaper sources of food. It will stimulate the growth of the urban economy, and will enable the accelerated expansion of agro-industry and hence of employment opportunities. It is believed that with rising rural incomes, the farming population will want to purchase more consumer goods as well as improved agricultural technology, and the increased demand for such goods will provide a further boost to industry, commerce and the service sectors.

Let us look briefly at the issue of land tenure and recent developments in this sector. The present government's land policy is for the most part similar to that of the Derg discussed above. What is significant in the present case is that land policy is now enshrined in the Constitution which entitles each adult in the rural areas that wishes to live by farming land sufficient for his/her livelihood; access to land for rural persons is thus a right. Land is here defined as the property of the people but is administered on their behalf by the state. In effect land is still state property, and peasants thus have only use rights over plots they have in their possession. This principle is reproduced in all *Killil* legislations. Land cannot be sold, exchanged or mortgaged, but the present policy does allow short term leasing or sharecropping as well as the hiring of labour, both of which were illegal under the Derg. The present land system has been criticised for many failings, among which are the following: the system promotes insecurity of tenure because it allows, among other things, periodic redistribution (or at least the threat of redistribution hangs over many peasants); it is inefficient because it constrains land transactions and has inhibited the emergence of a dynamic land market; it promotes fragmentation of land and growing pressure on land resources because it discourages rural people from leaving their farms for other employment opportunities, and it gives the state immense power over the farming population because land is state property.

A new measure which has recently been initiated and is in the process of being implemented in Wollaita as well as throughout the country is land certification. Each land user is issued a holding certificate describing the plot boundaries, size of land and including the names of the husband and wife who have a right of use. About half rural households have been issued with such certificates at present. Land certification is expected to promote greater security of holding and to encourage better land management practices. While the measure is a step in the right direction, we will have to wait and see if indeed it achieves its objectives. On the other hand, a Federal law issued in 2005 gives the woreda administration power to evict users from their holdings if the land is needed for public purposes as well as for investors. The compensation offered to the evicted user is much below the market value of the land. Peasants especially in peri-urban areas are being evicted to make way for investors in many parts of the country as well as SNNPR. In brief, the land user in the country as well as in Wollaita is still considerably insecure in his holdings and is thus discouraged from investing on the land and employing sound land management practices.

Agricultural-Led Development

The centrepiece of the agricultural development strategy is the package approach, mainly consisting of the dissemination of new agricultural technologies, in particular improved seeds, fertilisers and pesticides on the one hand, and providing improved extension services to promote the new technologies on the other. In more recent years, packages have been design for each of the main sectors of rural production: thus there is a crop package (fertilizer and improved seeds), a livestock package, a soil conservation package, etc. The strategy also calls for the expansion of small-scale irrigation schemes, and more recently water harvesting programs. Since the end of the 1990s, the government has focused almost single-mindedly on the promotion of these various "menu-based" integrated technology packages throughout the country. There is a strong focus on agricultural extension. The number of Development Agents (DAs) has been increased considerably since the mid-1990s, and in each locality these are required to help peasants choose the packages suitable for them and to demonstrate their benefits. There are now three DAs at each kebelle in Wollaita, each specialized on a different set of packages. The overall objective of the package approach is to improve food grain production in the shortest possible time, not just for purposes of food security but also surplus production to meet the requirements of the ADLI strategy discussed above. A new initiative to upgrade farmers' skill is the establishment of agricultural technology and vocational training centres which will eventually be located in each kebelle. The centres will use both classroom and field-based training and will issue at the end green certificates for each trainee. This program, when fully operational, is expected to equip farmers with knowledge of improved technologies and how to have access to them and to use them to their benefit.

Peasant farmers are expected to choose from a variety of menu-based packages the ones suitable for them. The packages are offered on credit to farmers, and the distribution of the inputs for the packages is handled by the cooperatives. Credit is interest free for those households involved in the safety net program, but others have to pay back the credit with interest. While in much of the country credit payment is often set at harvest time, in Wollaita payment collection has been distributed throughout the year. However, there is a great deal of credit default by peasants here who complain that they are unable to pay due to poverty and insufficient income. Since 2005, the Department of Agriculture and Rural Development (DARD) has been given the responsibility of implementing the government's new productive safety net program. The program identifies chronically food insecure households who are given employment opportunities to earn income (in kind or in cash) to enable them to achieve a minimum level of food security in the year. Food deficit households who are unable to work due to old age, infirmity and other reasons are given free food aid as long as they are in the program. The safety net program has been implemented in Wollaita for a year only (see Section 2.3.1 above).

As we can see from the data discussed in Section 2.3.1, there has not been any appreciable improvements in productivity since the new strategy was adopted over a decade ago. Fertilizer distribution in recent years has barely reached the level of the 1970s when WADU was actively engaged. Crop yields have not shown any appreciable improvements from those of the 1970s. The number of food deficit households dependent on food aid has been increasing since the 1990s. There are a variety of reasons why the extension-focused package approach has not been a flying success in Wollaita. To begin with, there are questions as to whether the packages are appropriate to the farming system in Wollaita. The specificity of this system has been discussed above and there is no need to repeat the arguments here. The Wollaita farming system must be seen along with the consequences of demographic stress noted earlier. Thus what is appropriate to the system in question is a technology that addresses the needs of the farming system and the problems of high population. The packages offered are obviously not designed with these twin objectives in mind. Secondly, there is an exclusive focus on technology, and there has not been an attempt to address problems other than inputs and farm practices. Farming in Wollaita is a complex undertaking with complex needs and demands. In addition, the technology approach has not given sufficient attention and failed to fully tap the experience and knowledge of peasant farmers.

Moreover, there has been a good deal of institutional instability. At the Federal level the Ministry of Agriculture (and now including Rural Development) and the corresponding offices at the Regional, Zonal and Kebelle levels have been reorganized numerous times since the EPRDF government assumed power. Institutional instability promotes inefficiency, discontinuities in program implementation, wastage of resources, low morale among staff, and loss of confidence on the part of the beneficiaries that the institution is set up to serve. In addition, there has been considerable staff turnover, a problem that, as we shall see further down, has been raised frequently by NGOs working in the area. Moreover, DAs and other extension personnel are often keen to leave the rural areas for better working conditions in the urban areas, thereby shirking their responsibilities. Overall, there are also questions as to whether the government has sufficient capacity to design innovative and relevant approaches and to implement these effectively. At present, Zonal DARD staff and their counterparts at the kebelle level are overstretched and spend much of their time on dealing with day-to-day problems without sufficient opportunity for effective long-term planning.

Food security has been a major problem in the country as well as in Wollaita since the present government came to power, and decision makers have given the problem considerable attention. The ultimate goal of the policy on food security that has evolved since the early 1990s is to achieve food self-sufficiency through the package programs noted above, but in the mean time, resettlement, water harvesting and the safety net program are expected to contribute towards this ultimate goal. The government's program of rural resettlement has been underway since the beginning of 2003, and, according to recent figures, some 500,000 people have already been moved to various locations in Amhara, Oromia, Tigrai and Southern *Killils*. In the course of three years, the program plans to settle 440,000 households or about 2.2 million people at an estimated cost of 217 million US dollars or 1.9 billion *Birr*. This is a massive program by any standard: it will constitute the largest relocation of population in this country. Table 8 provides a breakdown of the program in terms of population and cost by the participating *Killils*.

Table 8. Settlement areas, population and cost

Killil settlement site	No. of People	No. of HHs	Cost in Mn. birr
Tigrai: *Humera*	200,000	40,000	141
Amhara: *N. Gonder, Tsegede, Metema, Quara, TachArmachiho*	1,000,000	200,000	701
Oromia: *W. and E. Wollega, Illubabor, Jimma*	500,000	100,000	347
SNNPR: *Sheka, Kefa, Benchmaji, Dawro, Konta, S. Omo*	500,000	100,000	352
Total	**2,200,000**	**440,000**	**1541***

SOURCE: NCFSE 2003, Vol. II: 29; 22-25.

*The figure does not include 328 million Birr which is the cost of drugs and institutional capacity, warehouse and other costs, administration and contingency. The total is thus 1869 million birr.

The settlement program is viewed by the government as a lasting solution to chronic hunger and food insecurity on the one hand, and a way to meet the problem of land shortage on the other. The program, it is argued, will provide people in the vulnerable areas, who at present do not have sufficient land to grow enough to feed themselves, "access to improved land" in areas within their own *Killil* where there are "considerable amounts of land currently under-utilized" and "suitable for farm activities". Wollaita was the first in SNNPR to implement the government's settlement program. The program was launched in 2003 and the sites selected were located along the border with Sidama, including the Bilate area. Many of these sites were hotly contested by Sidama agro-pastoralists who claimed the land was theirs and being used for grazing purposes by them. As of 2005, the program had settled about 1270 hard-pressed peasants from different parts of Wollaita; however, over 40 percent of these soon left the settlement to return to their original homes due to a variety of problems including strong opposition by the Sidama (Mellese 2005). While there are still some settlers in some of the settlement sites, it is obvious that the settlement program in Wollaita was not a success and the resources spent on it would have been better utilized elsewhere.

Let us turn to the government's water harvesting program since water is an important issue in this discussion. The government launched a national campaign in early 2003 to accelerate rain water harvesting throughout the country. The objective of the program was to construct ponds and shallow wells for communities and households to enable them to have access to water in all seasons for agriculture and other uses. Water harvesting is one of the pillars of the government's food security strategy. In Wollaita the available evidence shows that a good number of ponds and wells have been constructed in some parts of the Zone. However, according to a national study conducted recently by the Federal government's own think tank, Ethiopian Development Research Institute (EDRI), many of these structures have become inadequate for a variety of reasons. The complaints raised by peasant users often are: the structures are subject to leakage and the walls of some have collapsed; there is siltation; they pose a serious health and safety hazard; there is rapid loss of water through high evaporation (Gezahegn et al. 2006). The structures have been constructed poorly, often by local DAs who were allocated a set number of structures to construct within a given time; this quota system means no serious attention was paid to the quality of the design and construction. On the other hand, small-scale irrigation schemes have been constructed in many parts of Wollaita by both government and NGOs. According to evidence from Department of Finance and Economic Development (DFED), the area covered by such schemes today is about 2,500 ha, serving almost 3,700 beneficiaries. Nearly half of the area covered by the schemes is in the lowlands of Damot Woyde, in the Bilate area. While this is a good beginning, what has been done so far is inadequate compared to the need of farmers in the Zone.

An important issue to raise here is the population issue and what has been done to address the problem in the Wollaita context. It has been over a decade since the government's population policy document has been issued; however, there have been very limited measures taken in terms of program implementation. The Federal population policy (1993) provides a broad framework within which Regional and Zonal governments are expected to undertake programs suitable to their needs. The goal of the policy is to reduce fertility substantially, to ensure that population growth is kept below economic growth through planned reduction of birth rates (including increased provision of contraceptives), and the balanced utilization of natural resources. A recent draft of the Zonal population program (2005b) has adopted this broad framework and suggests mainstreaming population issues into sectoral programs, such as health, education, and agriculture. Beyond this, there are virtually no measures undertaken by the government that are specifically grounded on the issue of high population growth. Obviously, the programs on safe sex and contraceptive distribution undertaken by the Health Department and NGOs in connection with HIV/AIDS prevention will have a birth control impact.

One of the main criticisms of the government's rural-centred and agricultural based development strategy is that it does not give sufficient attention to the urban sector. The question frequently asked is: how can peasant agriculture and the micro-agriculture of Wollaita in particular be the engine of economic growth in its present condition? As we have seen above, peasant farming is not showing any breakthroughs or even sufficiently high levels of improvements to escape grinding poverty. The Wollaita peasant is becoming more and more dependent on food aid and other assistance programs. In recent years, there are signs that the government is making a slight shift because it is beginning to provide more public funds to the urban areas. If this shift is real it is to be welcomed.

3.2 NGOs as Development Partners in Wollaita

3.2.1 NGOs in Wollaita

For our purposes here, we may take the mid-1980s as the beginning of NGO interventions in Wollaita *awraja*. Prior to this period, the Catholic and Protestant churches, which had a presence here going back to the 1920s, had built one or two schools and established heath services as part of their religious programs, particularly in the latter part of the 1940s and early 1950s, but these investments were modest in terms of their impact on the population. Following the virulent famine of the mid-1980s, which had a serious impact not only in the famine-prone north of the country but also in many of the *degga* and *woyna-degga* woredas of Wollaita, a number of NGOs, almost all of which were international organizations, started relief and later rehabilitation activities in the *awraja*.. The rules governing NGO activities at the time was for Relief and Rehabilitation Commission (RRC), the government's relief agency, to assign each of them a specific location or community to undertake programs, with the NGOs having no say in the matter. Thus in most cases, NGOs came to Wollaita not really because they had planned to but because they were posted there by the government.

All NGOs working in the country in this period were operating in a hostile policy environment: the Derg was suspicious of all independent organizations, seeing them either as posing an obstacle to its hard-line rural policies or as agents of foreign powers unfriendly to "socialist Ethiopia". Most NGOs, including those working in Wollaita, were not willing to support the Derg's radical programs of agricultural socialization, resettlement, and villagization, but neither were they in a position to voice criticism or express their concern. Yet they were working among the rural population which was the target of these programs and this was to pose a serious dilemma to many of them at the time. Some were reluctantly drawn into providing financial and other support to some of the programs on humanitarian grounds.

But NGOs working in Wollaita, as elsewhere in the country, were faced with many other dilemmas and difficulties. Many of them had no knowledge of the communities in which they found themselves. The shift from emergency relief to rehabilitation and finally to development was undertaken frequently without understanding the needs, or priorities of the communities concerned, and the resource base and social and economic opportunities available. On a good number of occasions, programs were launched either to secure funding, to satisfy donor requirements or because resources, in cash or in kind, were available for program operations. Soil and water conservation through food-for-work was a massive program in the 1980s supported by WFP and some of the major international donors, and a number of NGOs were quick to engage in conservation because the food was readily available. Moreover, most NGOs had a wide diversity of program interventions leading on occasions to making them seriously overstretched. Redd-Barna Ethiopia, for example, which was operational in Bolosso, was engaged in emergency response, agricultural development, environmental conservation, public health, education, water and sanitation, infrastructure, and capacity building at one and the same time.

Since the fall of the Derg, and particularly since the second half of the 1990s, the landscape of the voluntary sector in the country as well as in Wollaita has changed considerably. To begin with, there are now more voluntary organizations active both nationally and in the Zone than in the past. From a few hundred organizations in the country as a hole in the 1980s, their number has grown to more than two thousand, of which more than half are engaged in development programs. In Wollaita, there were not more than half a dozen organizations engaged in rehabilitation and development operations during the Derg; now there are close to twenty. Secondly, the composition of NGOs has changed, with the growth and increasing participation of indigenous NGOs both in emergency and development operations. During the Derg, there were only a handful of such organizations; at present they constitute more than half the total; in Wollaita nearly half the NGOs are home grown. Some of the larger international NGOs have withdrawn from operations and become donors.

Moreover, until recently, the voluntary sector was restricted to service delivery and issues related to advocacy, questions of policy relevance and demands for consultation on policy matters were all off limits. This has now changed to some extent and there are now advocacy, human rights and policy research organizations in the country. Thirdly, NGOs have learnt from the experiences of the past: they are now more focused in the delivery of services, relatively more knowledgeable about their constituency, and more responsive to local needs. They have realized that program diversity does not automatically spell success. Most organizations have now opted to take a more integrated and community-based approach. While each organization is now less overstretched than previously, still the programs run by NGOs in Wollaita are multifaceted

3.2.2 How Much Have NGOs Invested?

Before looking at the work of NGOs in Wollaita, let us examine briefly the larger picture at the national level. According to a recent information package on NGOs published by Christian Relief and Development Association (CRDA) and Disaster Prevention and Preparedness Commission (DPPC) (2004), between 1997 and 2001, NGOs working in the country invested 3.5 billion Birr, of which only 10 percent was spent on relief and rehabilitation, with the rest, i.e., 90 percent, going to a diversity of development programs. Table 9 shows the program components and the distribution of expenditure in this period.

Table 9. NGO expenditure for selected regions by sector (1997-2001) (in Million Birr)

Sector	*Amhara*	*Oromia*	*SNNPR*	*Tigrai*	*Total*
Food Security	197.55	267.31	165.44	179.95	948.49
Health/Water	131.53	361.00	325.16	68.69	991.28
HIV/AIDS	14.50	2.73	9.12	2.91	48.92
Education	101.49	234.07	130.54	84.54	700.75
Capacity Bldg	128.10	12.92	31.92	28.93	287.47
Infrastructure	96.87	36.57	28.52	12.47	209.37
Emergency	158.84	26.67	14.94	119.67	346.83
Total	**828.88**	**941.27**	**705.64**	**497.15**	**3533.11**

SOURCE: CRDA & DPPC 2004, p. 35.

Note: Total includes expenditures for Addis Ababa and Somalia Regions also.

The sectoral breakdown used in the document is unfortunate; putting health and water together is not a useful device. It would have been better, for our purposes, to have separated them, as will become clear later. Nevertheless, in SNNPR, Heath/Water is shown to have attracted the largest share of NGO investments. A close reading of the source publication shows actually that of the two, the health sector absorbed by far the biggest expenditure. Unfortunately, there is no data similar to this for Wollaita, and what is actually available is summarized in Table 10. All legally registered NGOs working in the Zone have to submit documents showing their program activities, plans and budgets to the Zonal Department of Finance and Economic Development (DFED) from which the information in the Table below is taken. The data in the Table may not be complete; there are a few NGOs operating in the Zone, such as for example SOS-Sahel, which have not been included.

Be that as it may, there are several points worth noting here. First is the fact that NGOs here are engaged in a diversity of programs, though which ones are the main beneficiaries of NGO funds is not easy to tell. Secondly, there is no information on emergency operations but we do know that there have been numerous emergency situations in Wollaita in the last five or ten years. Thirdly, we need to be careful in using the figures for the number of beneficiaries since there is double counting in some cases as the same people who are beneficiaries of different programs from the same NGO are counted more than once. Nevertheless, despite these caveats, it is clear that NGOs in Wollaita have brought into the area considerable resources and have benefited a large number of poor and needy people. According to the evidence, the 16 NGOs listed in the Table have spent 65.2 million Birr in 2005 in development operations covering all the seven woredas of the Zone. The investment is not equally spread in all woredas, the main highland woredas of Bolosso, Damot Gale and Soddo Zuria have been better served than the lowland woredas of Kindo Koysha, Humbo and Offa.

Table 10.   Information on NGOs operating in Wollaita (in 2005)

NGO	*Project component*	*Working in*	*Project budget* (Birr)	*Beneficiaries*
Acts of Compassion	Water Supply	Bolosso	500,000	400
Africa Humanitarian Action	Family planning, HIV/AIDS, Health	D.Gale, D. Woyde, Sodd Z, Bol	2,673,365	134,362
AMRC	Env, Disabled persons support	Sodd Z, Humbo	74,708	310
CCCE	Health	Sodd town	613,500	111
Concern	Food Sec, Family planning, Nutrition	D. Woyde	3,048,907	92,000
Day Star	Family Plan, Credit & Saving	D. Gale	694,127	---
InterAide Fr	Water, Agric, Health	D.Gale, Offa, Koysh	782,852	3260
Int. Medical Co	Health	D.Gale	11,731,683	4130
MFTA	Health	All woredas	1,997,102	25,364
Orbis	Eye Care	Sodd town	662,716	6,062
Soddo Hosana Catholic	Ed, Health, Credit, HIV/AIDS	All woredas	8,575,515	132,964
Terepeza Dev Assoc	Family health, Children, Food sec	D.Gale, Bol, Koysh, Sodd twn	4,306,451	11,968
Wollaita Dev Assoc	Food sec, Water, Ed, Health, HIV	All woredas	7,530,717	---
Wollaita Tussa	Culture, Sport	Sodd town	377,900	---
Wonta Dev Assoc	Food, Ed, Helath, Credit	D. Woyde	11,395,583	8,814
World Vision	Food sec, Water, Health, Ed	Soddo Z, Humbo	8,401,054	298,844
Total			**65,193,213**	**763,753**

Source: DFED (2005)

Note: AMRC: Arba Minch Rehabilitation Center; CCCE: Children's Cross Connection Eth; MFT: Mossy Foot Prevention & Treatment Association.

The most current information from the files of the same Department (compiled after the publication of the source for Table 10) contains a slightly different data. Here, the total fund "utilized" in 2005 by seventeen NGOs (Lutheran World Federation which is shown to have spent 1.4 million Birr is the addition) working in the Zone is put at 48.7 million Birr, while the budget earmarked for the same year is given as 70.9 million. On the other hand, the data file also states that the total planned budget for the duration of the projects of each of the seventeen NGOs, from 2002 to 2009 (ranging from three to five years, depending on each particular case) adds up to more than 145 million Birr. Figures for the 1990s are not available because until 2000, Wollaita was not a Zone and its seven woredas were part of North Omo. It is worth noting that even if we take the lower expenditure figure of 48.7 million Birr, NGOs have spent as much money in one year as WADU spent in its twelve years of work in Wollaita.

For comparison, a look at the funds spent by individual NGOs may indicate the magnitude of the resource flow into the area. Let us take the case of World Vision. This organization has been operating in Wollaita since the 1985 famine. After engaging in emergency relief and rehabilitation programs during the first four years, it launched an integrated development program, called Area Development Program (ADP) focusing on household food security in 1990. Its two separately managed ADPs, based in Soddo Zuria and Humbo woredas, have undertaken a wide variety of projects including the construction of a large number of schools, water supply schemes, health, agricultural and livestock improvement activities, and basic infrastructure. Figures provided to the study team by the staff of Soddo Zuria ADP shows that since the launch of the development program in 1990, and excluding the relief and rehabilitation activities before then, this ADP alone has invested 5.2 million USD, or the equivalent of over 40 million Birr in the woreda. Moreover, the ADP was also responsible for managing (under separate funding and financial management) a nutrient and health program called MICAH, and a food-for-work program called DAP. Both these programs (funded by Canadian CIDA and USAID, respectively) have now been phased out after being run in the area for over six years. The total budget expenditure for the MICAH program was 512,734 USD and the DAP program 91,539 USD. A third program similarly managed with separate funding but now phased out was a scheme to popularize new poultry breeds; this program invested 543,900 USD. The three separate programs thus have spent 1.2 million USD in the six years that they were implemented. If we add this to the regular expenditure of Soddo Zuria ADP shown above, the organization's investment in the woreda in the years since 1990 comes to 6.4 million USD, or about 55 million Birr. On the other hand, figures provided by the World Vision Ethiopia head office in Addis Ababa shows that from 1999 to 2006, Soddo Zuria and Humbo ADPs had spent a total of over 12 million USD which is equivalent to 104 million Birr. By any standards, this is a considerable investment.

Because of the lack of reliable information I have not been able to determine the full extent of NGO investment in Wollaita in the two decades since the 1980s, but I believe the evidence available, incomplete as it is, suggests that all NGOs combined (i.e., those engaged in the Zone in the past as well as today) may have spent between 200 and 250 million Birr in program activities in these years. This is obviously only a rough estimate and should not be taken as accurate or definitive. Which sectors have attracted the greater share of NGO investments and have benefited the most people? This question is important because the answer gives an indication of the development priorities set or accepted by the voluntary sector in Wollaita. But unfortunately the question is not an easy one to answer largely because the available data is not sufficiently disaggregated by sector and because of the points raised above. If we take financial outlay alone as the main criteria, there may be a bias in favor of one sector or another. For example, water development schemes, particularly those serving agricultural purposes (small irrigation, etc.) are relatively very expensive, hence water outlays appear high in the annual budgets, but the programs may only serve a small number of beneficiaries. Should one use instead the number of beneficiaries served by a given investment? There are difficulties here too, one of which has been raised earlier. Nevertheless, taking these difficulties into account, a provisional identification of priority areas will be useful for our purposes and for the debate that this study hopes to promote. Based on the data from DFED noted above, discussions with concerned NGO staff as well as publications from these organizations, I find that the sectors which have attracted the biggest share of NGO investments in Wollaita are the following (in order of importance):

> Health. This includes construction and rehabilitation of health posts, clinics and hospitals; improvement of health care services; reproductive health and family planning; HIV/AIDS; counseling services, health staff training and support.

> Agriculture/Food security. This includes improvement of agricultural practices, provision of new inputs and crop varieties; farmer trainings; livestock development, veterinary services and cattle disease control; soil and water conservation

> Water. a) construction and rehabilitation of boreholes, wells, and hand pumps; spring protection; roof run-off conservation; b) water harvesting schemes; small scale irrigation; small to medium dam construction. Those activities listed under (a) are mainly for domestic consumption while those under (b) primarily for agricultural use. Moreover, water development frequently includes sanitation programs, which has meant improved latrines and better personal and environmental hygiene.

> Education. Construction and rehabilitation of schools; school feeding programs; support to improved educational materials.

There are a number of significant issues that may be worth noting in this connection. While the attention given to the health needs of rural communities is to be appreciated, the attention given to reproductive health and especially to family planning is a cause for serious concern. In the light of the immense population pressure in the Zone and the fact that demographic growth is alarmingly high, more attention should have gone to health support programs that address this problem. We shall return to this further down. A number of NGOs are addressing the problem of HIV/AIDS, and this does have a birth control dimension; still, in view of the enormity of the population problem, priority in health matters should have been given to addressing the issue. Moreover, both at the national and Killil levels (Table 10 above) as well as in Wollaita, the resources allocated to fighting HIV/AIDS is not commensurate with the gravity of the problem. Secondly, given the gravity and frequency of drought, far more NGOs should have been investing in water development than is the case at present. Among the organizations that have phased out their programs from the area, Action for Development and Oxfam GB may be cited for their considerable investment in water development. Of those which are still engaged in the area, Acts of Compassion, Inter Aide France, SOS-Sahel and World Vision have a strong focus on water. World Vision has constructed the Lekemse Water Project which has a reservoir built near Soddo town and which brings clean water to the population of Humbo woreda some 35 kms away, with outlets along the way for irrigation and domestic consumption.

3.2.3 Achievements

The NGO presence in Wollaita extends for over twenty years though most of the organizations active now are relatively new to the area. Organizations such as World Vision and CONCERN came here in the mid-1980s, and SOS-Sahel began in 1990, but the rest have a shorter history. On the other hand, there have been more than half a dozen other organizations which were actively engaged here but have since phased out their programs for a variety or reasons. The question now is: what has been the impact of NGOs as development partners in Wollaita? Is it possible to design an accurate or even acceptable yardstick to measure the contributions of NGOs to development and poverty reduction in the area? This is a very difficult question to answer since "impact" in the complex circumstances existing in the area, and given the paucity of relevant and reliable data, is very hard to measure with any degree of accuracy. And yet, the question has to be addressed because it is pertinent to our case. Perhaps one way of "measuring" impact would be to reverse the question and ask: what would have happened in rural Wollaita in these twenty years if NGOs had not been present in the area? We know that many thousands of lives were saved during the recurrent emergencies thanks to the timely intervention by NGOs. Many poor households were able to recover from emergencies, to recoup their loses, build assets, and have access to health, education, and water supply services due to the development programs in their communities undertaken by NGOs.

The available data clearly shows that the NGO presence in Wollaita has been quite positive and the Organizations have played and continue to play an important role in addressing the complex problems of development and poverty reduction in the area. Let us look at some of the tangible and "intangible evidence. Table 10 above shows that 763,753 people benefited from the development programs run by NGOs in 2005; this is about half the population of the Zone. While the accuracy of the figure may be contested it is evident nevertheless that the outreach of the organizations has been quite considerable. There are other tangible evidences of impact scattered in many rural communities and in all woredas, of which the main ones are:

➢ a large number of small scale irrigation schemes have been built and are in use by communities, and these have contributed to farmers' resilience against recurrent drought and helped improve agricultural income and food security; in this connection, the importance of the control of the tse tse fly and the deadly diseases associated with it by NGOs working in the lowland woredas cannot be underestimated;

➢ scores of health facilities, schools, and water supply schemes have been provided thus contributing to better health services, higher school enrollment and improved well-being for rural communities;

➢ many rural access roads and more than a dozen bridges have been constructed making the movement of people and goods and access to social services easier and more efficient;

> considerable investment has been made to promote soil and water conservation and to rehabilitate degraded environments; these are clearly visible in many areas, and their contribution to improved food and livestock production is obvious.

But it is also important to look at the intangible outcomes, and because sometimes these may be more significant in the long run than the physical assets noted above. Of these, the most significant are the self-managed socio-economic institutions that NGOs have helped rural communities to establish which have become sustainable, enabling peasants to improve their income and have access to credit services. The main examples to be cited here are the variety of self-managed community-based cooperative societies, water users associations, credit and savings schemes, micro-enterprises, and livestock improvement initiatives that are all being successfully managed by peasants and local communities themselves. Some development practitioners may put more value in these successes than the physical assets put in place, because such successes are evidence of important knowledge gained by rural communities. The ability of poor people to manage their own affairs by learning new skills and adopting new institutions is an indicator of local empowerment which is a significant asset in development and poverty reduction.

3.2.4 Shortcomings

And yet, the fundamental problems of *poverty and destitution on the one hand, and the vulnerability of communities and households on the other remain serious and may even be worsening from year to year*. Let us re-examine, in this regard, the NGO record in the light of the "prime movers" of poverty discussed earlier in this study and the extent to which the programs undertaken by the voluntary sector are significant in this context. I have argued above that unless development interventions address these primary causes with significant positive results, not much progress in livelihood improvement and poverty reduction will be achieved in real terms. I believe the NGO record is by and large deficient in this regard. While most of the NGOs are clearly aware of the root causes of poverty and destitution and there is broad consensus that these have to be tackled in a sustained manner, the development programs implemented by them have not given sufficient attention to the problems in question.

The first prime cause is the demographic challenge and the closely linked problem of land and resource shortage. The causal relationship between demography and land is that there is extreme land shortage because there are far too many people on the land. How much effort has been made by the voluntary sector to address the demographic problem and the Malthusian crisis hanging over Wollaita society? The answer in brief is: not much. The standard program undertaken in this regard is family planning which involves counseling, and the provision of birth control services to women who are willing to participate in the program. Nevertheless, family planning programs have not been part of development interventions by mainstream NGOs, and it still does not command serious attention. The program has only been undertaken on a sufficient scale by a very small number of NGOs only in the last five to six years, of which Africa Humanitarian Action (AHA) is the main organization fully engaged in it and related issues of reproductive health and HIV/AIDS prevention. AHA, which works in five of the most densely populated woredas of Wollaita, provides counseling, information and education, and birth control services through its community based agents. According to the project manager in Soddo, there is widespread awareness of the need for family planning in the rural areas, the main problem is service delivery and the choice of services. Until recently, the family planning coverage in the Zone was only two percent, but currently AHA estimates that coverage has increased to 15 percent. This is woefully inadequate relative to the immense problem of population pressure and high fertility.

The second causal factor has to do with urbanization and development interventions in the urban areas. Our findings show that the primary focus of almost all development activities undertaken by NGOs is the rural population. The urban areas have by and large been neglected except for small scale undertakings involving health and, though not shown here, credit and microfinance. While some of the population of the smaller towns have benefited from the spill-over effects of rural development, particularly having to do with health, water and education programs, there have been few *substantive* development interventions by NGOs in the urban sector. Many NGO officials interviewed for this study are of the opinion that the voluntary sector has to give greater attention to the urban areas and urban-focused programs will have to be carefully formulated. The third factor is livelihood diversification. The NGO record here is relatively better though by no means adequate relative to the scale of the problem, nor a cause for celebration. A good number of NGO programs have addressed the need for increased household income from a diversity of sources, and here the main approach has been to support income generating activities through micro-enterprise development, saving and credit schemes or support to community-based cooperative organizations.

The last causal factor to be examined in the light of the NGO record is the frequency of drought and its complex repercussions. The standard remedy often employed is the amelioration of its impact through emergency operations in which all NGOs have been involved in one way or another. However, there has also been an awareness that water development is of central importance but, as has been noted above, NGO investment on water is inadequate, and the total investment on it, including that of government, is not commensurate with the gravity of the problem to be addressed,. It is my considered opinion that massive investment in sound and sustainable water development schemes is necessary in order to free peasant farmers from dependence on rainfall and the vagaries of nature. All partners engaged in development programs in Wollaita, government, non-government and private sector partners will have to work together to achieve this goal

3.2.5 Challenges

What has been the challenges faced by NGOs in Wollaita? These may be grouped into three broad categories: attitudinal, institutional and managerial. The first challenge is a product of historical circumstances: that NGOs came to Wollaita in the 1980s to do emergency work and were seen by the people as "aid givers" has left an enduring legacy that has proven difficult to shake off. The relationship between NGOs and their beneficiaries is still informed by the notion, if not reality, of "aid giving" which makes the tasks of the organizations quite difficult. Many initiatives to enable peasants and their communities to take over responsibility for managing health, water, savings and credit schemes have failed as a result of this. The relief – rehabilitation – development continuum remains strong today and it is difficult if not impossible for an NGO not to be involved in relief. The problem is compounded by the fact that the rural poor are increasingly dependent on public support systems and food aid.

The institutional problems are much more complex. First, there is the relationship between government on the one hand and NGOs on the other. While compared with the Derg period, the policy environment governing NGO activities has improved to some extent, there are still numerous challenges and obstacles on the way.

To begin with, all NGO officials that we interviewed for this study were unanimous in their view that NGOs are not considered as important development partners by the government. While there have been frequent workshops involving government and NGO staff, the outcome of these meetings has not often been very fruitful: they have not led to much genuine effort at greater partnership or closer consultation and involvement of NGOs in development planning and decision making. There are three important committees at the woreda level where it is important for NGOs to participate. These are the Woreda Development, Disaster Preparedness and Prevention, and Safety Net Committees. Most of the NGO officials we talked to felt that NGOs were either not participating in these committees or that their participation was less than satisfactory because their involvement was not actively sought by the authorities.

Related to this is the issue of what NGOs described as the high staff turnover among government employees, both senior and middle-tier, at the woreda and Zonal level. Sometimes public officials are transferred elsewhere or choose to move to other posts soon after they have benefited by training and other opportunities provided by NGOs. Such high turnover has a damaging impact on program implementation, and sustainability of project plans, leading to delays, inefficiency and wastage of scarce resources on the part of the organizations.

The second major challenge is the relationship among NGOs themselves. There was a good deal of consensus among the NGOs interviewed that there was not much networking within the voluntary sector, that there was a great deal of duplication of effort, and hardly any coordination of activities or strategic collaboration among them. Each organization is working by itself, without much effort at experience sharing and harmonization of approaches and working practices with organizations working in the same area.

Finally, another important managerial challenge that has been raised in several NGO documents is the problem of staff turnover within the organizations themselves. There are considerable difficulties attracting high caliber staff to work in the rural areas. The further removed the project site is from Addis Ababa or other big urban centers, the more difficult it is to attract and keep skilled and experienced staff.

3.3 Urban Areas and the Private Sector

At the time of our field visit we conducted a rapid and informal survey of businesses in Soddo. The results are shown in the table below. Street vendors, traditional home made food and drink shops have been excluded.

Table 11. The Private Sector in Soddo (2006)

Retail and wholesale shops		Metal, wood, mills, etc.	
*Souq*s (petty retailing)	1129	Wood works	278
Tailoring and clothes	760	Metal works	121
Groceries	59	Garages	54
Bakeries	101	Tyre repair	11
Butcheries	56	Flour mills	28
Grain stores	98	Petrol station	5
Music & video	90	***Crafts and skills***	
Photo	18	Barber shops	114
Drug stores	67	Beauty shops	71
Stationery	134	Weavers shops	155
Electric shops	75	Smithing	5
Building materials	63	***Manufacturing***	
Hotels, food, bars		Factory	1
Restaurants	243		
Bars	109		
Pastries	20		
Small hotels	57		
Large hotels	17		
Tea rooms	289		

SOURCE: Informal survey of Soddo, 2006.

As can be seen from the survey, Soddo is predominantly a service centre rather than a provider of industrial and other employment. The great majority of the businesses are petty, family-run enterprises which employ not more than three to five people each. In addition, there was some construction work going on in the town, offering employment largely to the urban unemployed. There is of course a sizable number of civil servants in Soddo and the other towns. Since Wollaita became a self-managing Zone, the number of civil servants in the capital has increased; there has been a comparable increase in the woredas as well. At present there are nearly 6,300 public employees in the Zone. Be that as it may,

Soddo in its present state cannot provide many opportunities for employment to the rural population.

There is no city in Wollaita larger than Soddo, which at present is said to have a population close to 60,000. According to DFED, the total urban population of the Zone for 2005 is estimated to be about 135,000. Of these only three towns, Soddo, Boditi and Areka have a population of over 20,000. The rest are small urban settlements with less than 5,000 inhabitants each (except Bele which has a little over 6,000). Needless to say, the state of business in all these towns is considerably poorer than that of Soddo. Thus, at present, the urban sector is too poor, too underdeveloped to serve as a catalyst for rural growth and a magnet for employment to hard pressed peasants. At present, the towns are suffering from large-scale unemployment, and any slight improvement in the economy will largely go to benefit, at least initially, the urban unemployed. Nevertheless, we should not forget that however small it may be, the growth of urban centers has had a beneficial impact on rural production. There is a growing demand for food and other agricultural products that some of the more enterprising peasants, specially in the peri-urban areas, are taking advantage of. There is no information showing the economic impact of the larger towns on the farming population around them but it must be quite considerable.

On the other hand, the view from the countryside is that living in town is better than living in the rural areas. One of the questions we asked peasants during the rural interviews we held was this: what would you do if you were given a free gift of 100,000 Birr without any strings attached? The answers we received were quite interesting and have important policy implications. Almost all respondents said they would invest in economic activities which would enable them to live in town or closely associate them with it. The following were the preferences that emerged (in order of importance):

> ➢ Engage in the hotel and restaurant business in town

> ➢ Invest in modern farming with tractors

> ➢ Buy a heavy truck and do business in the transport sector

> ➢ Open a retail shop *(souq)* in town

> ➢ Build a nice house in town

> ➢ Open a rural drug store and do business in the health sector

> ➤ Buy oxen and fatten them for the market; engage in large-scale grain trade.

In a rural survey I and other colleagues conducted in northern Ethiopia for a study in 2000 we asked peasants the same kind of question, and the answers we got were very similar. Clearly, *many peasants will gladly escape from the world of small scale farming if they were given the opportunity*. None of the peasants in this or the earlier study said they would invest the money on their farms, their homesteads, their livestock, poultry, etc. The only exception to this is the preference shown by some for cattle fattening, obviously for the urban market.

From interviews with officials at the Zonal Department of Trade, Industry, and Urban Development, we gathered that the climate for business and investment has improved in recent years, although some of the businessmen we talked to in Soddo thought the improvement was not adequate enough. The Department is responsible for development programs outside agriculture. Its main objective is to encourage the private sector, attract investment, reduce urban unemployment through miro-enterprises and address the housing problem in the urban areas. Both Soddo and Boditi have established enterprise zones to attract investors. Our informants at the Department pointed out that since 2004 many investors from other parts of the country, as well as one foreign investor have come to Wollaita to invest in hotels and tourism, modern farming and agro-industry, and real estate and construction enterprises. The Department has approved 140 investment applications worth some 597 million Birr with employment opportunities for over 10,000 people. Of these, a good number have already started operations or are in the process of doing so.

The other important program of the Department is micro-enterprise development, a program aimed at reducing poverty and unemployment. The government has designed a variety of packages such as woodwork, metal work, and construction packages in which participating individuals are trained. The process involves the urban unemployed setting up package-based cooperatives which are then provided training and offered credit opportunities for their operations. The trainers are industrial development extension agents who will in the future be trained at business and small enterprise training centers now being built in the three big towns in the Zone. So far a few thousand urban unemployed have benefited by the micro-enterprise program.

We interviewed several important businessmen in Soddo and asked them about the business climate and the opportunities for private sector investment. Almost all pointed out that while there have been some encouraging improvements there are still considerable obstacles for businessmen. Among the main ones noted were red tape within government agencies responsible for approving applications for investment, lack of sufficient goodwill by the Zonal government to the private sector, and bureaucratic hurdles to obtain credit from government-owned banks.

Most local businessmen get access to investment capital not through formal financial institutions, but through the traditional *iqoub*, and family and friends. These sources, and especially *iqoub* are easy to access and provide funds quickly enough to enable the investor to efficiently exploit emerging opportunities. However, the capital available through such means is small to medium and because of this and government red tape, many businesses have been forced to invest in sectors that are already crowded and provide limited employment. On the other hand, the fact that labor is cheap and plentiful was seen as a positive factor for business activity. The main sectors identified as being good for investment were hotels and tourism, modern farming (specially growing high valued industrial crops), and agro-industry.

It was the opinion of the businessmen that the private sector can play an important role in poverty reduction. A healthy business enterprise could provide increasing employment opportunities which will be important in tackling unemployment and reducing poverty. The private sector can stimulate rural production through a strong demand for agricultural products and by offering both consumer products and employment. The businessmen felt that government policy has neglected both the private and urban sectors, though they saw some signs of a change in this regard in recent years. The private sector can also be an important partner to government: the public sector cannot do everything and it needs partners to share its burdens.

IV. Conclusions and Policy Implications

4.1 Summing Up

The foregoing analysis has examined the existing conditions and livelihood situation, reviewed the efforts on the part of government and development partners to promote development and tackle poverty, and raised a number of issues that we hope will provide ample opportunities for debate and reflection. Obviously, due to space limitations, and limitations of time and resources, a good deal of detail and considerable subject areas had to be left out or noted only briefly. In the remaining pages we shall discuss the conclusions that emerge from our analysis and suggest issues and subject areas that we believe are significant for policy debates and advocacy work.

Over the last four decades there have been two main actors and a third minor actor that have made significant efforts to stimulate development and tackle the problem of poverty in Wollaita. The first two are government and voluntary organizations, and the third the private sector. The long and arduous struggle of the farming population itself is of course notable but has been given much less attention due to the terms of reference for this study. It is hoped that others will redress this imbalance at an opportune time.

Over the last four and half decades considerable effort has been made and immense resources invested in Wollaita by all actors combined. The achievements are by no means insignificant. Since the 1960s, when Wollaita was almost totally neglected, a good deal of investment in basic infrastructure has been made. There is an extensive network of roads linking all the woredas and their towns as well as reaching a large number of rural communities. In this regard, Wollaita is far ahead of many areas of the country. There is a modern (by Ethiopian standards) communications network, and electric power supply, a relatively vigorous transport system, a growing number of financial institutions, and clean water supply for many of the urban centers. The urban centers have grown from two tiny settlements at the time of the Dejazmach to three bigger towns and more than half a dozen smaller towns- admittedly, not a dramatic growth but growth all the same.

In terms of social services, considerable progress has been made relative to the situation in the 1960s in terms of school enrollment, health coverage, agricultural extension, and marketing. At present, official figures show that 82 percent of children of 1st to 4th grades are attending school, 58 percent for those of 5th to 8th grades. At present, there are two institutions of higher learning in Soddo and a new university is being built. Health coverage is said to have reached 44 percent, although a high proportion of this is serving urban areas. Extension work, if measured by the number of extension agents has expanded considerably. There is one DA for every 350 farm households. While the growth rate has stagnated, there are far more households using modern inputs and improved agricultural practices today than in the 1960s. All these are, by Ethiopian standards, essential elements of modernity. Hence, in many ways, Wollaita is different today than it was four and half decades ago.

And yet, the problems of poverty and destitution, unemployment, disease, food insecurity, resource loss, in brief extreme rural hardship and suffering not only persist but have increased in magnitude and severity. Here is an apparent paradox: modernity is in progress (though very slowly) in Wollaita but it is accompanied by greater poverty and destitution, and increased suffering and hardship for the rural population as we have shown in earlier chapters. A small proportion of the population has benefited from the development programs of the preceding decades and that and that alone has been the economic and livelihood significance of modernity in Wollaita.

4.2 Policy Implications

Any policy discussion must of course be framed within commonly accepted principles of democratic practice. Asked what the solution to Wollaita's problems are, many informants raised a number of issues in this regard, including the need for peasant empowerment, the adoption of a bottom-up approach instead of the customary top-down approach, commitment, transparency and accountability on the part of public officials, and consultation with local communities on matters affecting their lives. Peasants suggested that listening to the voices of the people from below and effective monitoring of program implementation were significant solutions to existing problems. In presenting the recommendations noted below I do not mean to indicate that these are not important. On the contrary, peasant empowerment and democratic practice are essential. My purpose here is to select priority issues that are specific to the development problematic of Wollaita.

As we have tried to show earlier, the development interventions have by and large failed to address the key determinants of poverty and destitution we have noted at the outset of this discussion, though the failure is greater or lesser in degree depending on the problems and policy interventions concerned. Without repeating the discussions presented above, we shall briefly review our main arguments as follows:

Demographic stress and resource scarcity. The immense population pressure in the countryside has brought about severe land shortage and deterioration of the resource base as well as the farming system and land management practices. None of the development interventions discussed in this work made a concerted effort and committed resources commensurate with the gravity of the problem to address this issue. Unless a substantial proportion of the rural population is induced through economic, financial and other incentives, to move out of agriculture and the rural areas, and unless through this means land is released for much bigger operations, and the holdings of farmers, specially enterprising farmers, are increased four to five fold or more, agriculture will continue to stagnate and rural poverty and destitution will continue to grow. Land is scarce and holdings are miniscule because there are far too many people on the land. Reduce the demographic pressure and there will be more land accessible to farmers. Changing the farming system, which will be a desirable end in the longer term, will be easier when holdings are larger. Greater holdings will change the dense settlement pattern that is so characteristic of rural Wollaita today.

Many people interviewed for this study have raised the subject of settlement as a possible solution to land shortage. Both the Derg and the present government have attempted to employ settlement schemes to address the problem of food insecurity and resource shortage. But I believe resettlement will NOT solve the problems we are dealing with. To begin with, settlement at the macro level is simply moving farmers from one farm location to another. As soon as the so-called vacant space is filled we are back to the same problem. Secondly, I have argued elsewhere that few resettlement schemes have been successful, and that the program does not solve the fundamental problems for which it was designed but only postpones the day of reckoning. There are very few "unoccupied" lands in the country, fewer still in Wollaita suitable for peasant agriculture. But more important for our purposes is the argument that we have proposed here: the aim should be to move people out of agriculture, not from one agricultural site to another. There are far too many small farmers in Wollaita and in the country as a whole: what we need is fewer farmers and larger holdings. Larger holdings will encourage farmers to try new technologies, to take risks to innovate, to adopt conservation techniques, and to employ sound land management practices.

The immediate question to follow from this is: what will happen to the population removed from agriculture? There are no ready answers but this is the kind of question that has NOT been discussed extensively and in depth in this country. I do not have a panacea to offer or a magic wand to solve the problem, but I believe this should be a subject for extended public debate, reflection and in-depth research. Perhaps the subject needs to be examined in conjunction with the next issue to be raised here.

Urbanization and urban demand. Wollaita is one of the least urbanized Zones in the country. There is sufficient evidence to show that the greater the rural population in a country the poorer that country is. The poorest countries in UNDP's World Development Index are also the least urbanized. The reverse of this is that the greater the urban population in a country relative to the rural, the better-off the country is.

It is well known that the arbiters of the rural economy are often the urban centers, unless there is a major export market siphoning off rural produce. It is the urban demand that drives the market for the rural surplus and determines in the end the cropping strategy of the farm families. Urban demand adds value to rural labor and production. And urban demand is determined by the size of the urban population. A greater number of urban people will mean more demand for food and other agricultural products. Moreover, as the urban population grows not only in size but economically, that is, as it becomes wealthier, it adds further value to farm work through increased demand for agricultural products. Thus the following observations follow and are presented for debate:

> ➢ Each increase in the urban population adds more demand for food and other farm products.

> ➢ This will add value to rural work specially if the urban population is increasing faster than the rural population. Hence, greater rural to urban migration is essential. The government's population policy discourages this kind of migration, which we believe is ill advised.

> ➢ Increased rural investment is made possible as rural production benefits by increased urban demand.

> ➢ Thus, urban development fuels rural economic progress. Urban development involves greater investment in the urban sector giving rise to expanded employment, better social services, modern communication, transport, and power supply infrastructure.

Livelihood diversification. The importance of livelihood diversification to improvements in rural income has now come to be recognized, but programs that encourage such diversification have not been adequate under the policies of all three regimes. Diversification goes hand in hand with appropriate institutions that are needed for it. The major constraint here is access to credit, and appropriate technology, and the ability to identify niche products in which local communities and Wollaita as a whole has a comparative advantage. There is limited benefit to be gained if one is to encourage all women, for instance, to take up sheep fattening or to sell local home brew. The spread of micro-finance institutions is a step in the right direction. Peasants have no opportunities for credit from the formal credit services such as banks, hence alternative sources of credit accessible to ordinary households are urgently needed.

Recurrent drought. Many respondents have pointed to the frequency of drought and poor rains as being responsible for the poor performance of agriculture and frequent food shortages. Food crises are brought on by poverty and drought only becomes a contributing factor when the farmer is poor to begin with. But, as we have seen earlier, Wollaita peasants are poor or destitute and the occurrence of even minor variations in the rains and the environment leads to the collapse of livelihoods. I believe the appropriate intervention one needs to consider in this regard is how *to free peasant cultivators from dependence on rainfall*. As we have seen, the development interventions of the past have not made sufficient investment in water development schemes though some programs have been undertaken in the water sector. What is needed at present is *massive investment in water development to enable large numbers of farmers to be less dependent on rainfall and the vagaries of nature.* This means extensive construction of small-scale irrigation schemes, of small dams, ponds, wells, cisterns, spring protection and capping, rainfall collection schemes, and technologies that go with such programs. But such investment must be preceded by a careful and thorough assessment of the water resource potential of Wollaita.

4.3 The Way Forward

Here I would like to point to the basic elements of a new policy framework and the bases of debate that this work will hopefully stimulate.

i)   There should be a shift of development policy by all actors concerned, specially government and development partners, to give greater attention to the acute problems fuelled by population growth, demographic stress and the concomitant crisis of land shortage. The demographic problem is an urgent one and serious and sustained debate on it is essential. Development partners need to conduct sensitization and advocacy programs on it as soon as possible. What is demanded is not a relocation of the rural population from one farm environment to another but a shift of population out of the agricultural sector and the rural areas. The problem of resource degradation in general and soil erosion and soil fertility decline in particular cannot be effectively tackled under the current system of micro-holdings and micro-agriculture.

ii) Relieving the population pressure must mean greater rural-to-urban migration and the growth of the importance of the urban sector to both the rural and overall economy. The urban areas in partnership with rural farmers must be the engine of economic progress. At present, urban Wollaita is too weak and too underdeveloped to serve as the flagship of economic progress in the area. Hence, considerable investment in the urban sector is needed but here partnership between the public and private sector must be made the cornerstone of progress in urban development. The voluntary sector must also give greater attention to the urban areas than it has done up to now. There are diverse opportunities for advocacy work in this regard.

iii) Innovative approaches must be formulated to expand opportunities for livelihood diversification. Niche products for niche markets need to be identified to give local communities comparative advantage and hence greater benefits from supplementary income generation activities.

iv) The fight against environmental shocks, particularly drought and rainfall variability must not be confined to food aid and public and private support programs. *I believe the issue is freeing farmers from exclusive reliance on rainfall.* This will have to involve sound and extensive investment in the water sector.

v) In the course of this study a number of informants raised the problems of aid dependency and the lack of a saving culture among peasants as cause for concern. We need a series of well-grounded studies to determine what the nature, extent and bases of these problems are before prescribing the appropriate medicine. However, until such evidence is available we should benefit from experiences already at hand. I believe an extended advocacy work needs to be undertaken to promote self-managed, local organizations in the rural areas. There are a number of successful local organizations, such as multi-purpose or savings and credit cooperatives, and water users associations, initiated by NGOs but now fully self-managed in many parts of the rural areas. This experience needs to be shared with others and replicated widely. Such independent organizations help to empower peasants to manage their own affairs. It has been shown that with careful training and monitoring during the initial period, poor peasants can manage their own organizations. The failure of most of the cooperatives during the WADU period was the absence of such training and supervision. Self-managed local organizations are important means of promoting self-reliance and breaking the dependency syndrome now said to be strongly entrenched. The absence of a saving culture that some informants are worried about needs to be examined carefully. Here the role micro-finance institutions are now playing, not just in providing access to credit but in encouraging savings should be singled out for appraisal. But the institutions are thinly spread in the countryside and serve only a limited number of the needy. Advocacy work here too should aim to extend the services of such institutions by creating more of them and extending their reach. At present there are only two micro-finance institutions in Wollaita but there should be much more.

vi) Finally, let us return to the voluntary sector and how best to make its contributions more effective. At present, the customary practice is for each NGO to work largely by itself, in isolation within a given locality and without much cooperation and coordination of effort with others. There is considerable duplication of work, limited sharing of experiences and best practices, a lack of a culture of learning from other organizations working for the same cause, and few attempts at harmonization of approaches, strategies and working practices. I believe the NGO community in Wollaita could make a more effective contribution to the fight against poverty and the improvement of livelihoods if there was greater coordination of work and cooperation within it. What the nature of the cooperation should be will have to be determined through wide debate and advocacy work within the voluntary sector itself.

There are attempts by NGOs in some areas of the country to form some kind of close working alliance or association to enhance their effectiveness. Coordination of effort or cooperation can take many forms, some of which may be:

> division of responsibility based on expertise and program experience;

> division of responsibility based on location or constituency;

> closer consultation and harmonization of working practices, strategies, approaches;

> avoidance of duplication of work which would be facilitated by closer consultation, and others.

During the interviews we held with NGOs there was broad consensus on many of the problems cited and the need for greater cooperation. But there were different opinions as to how this could be achieved. Many noted that the government should have a strong role in bringing the NGO community together, and that this could be done through greater recognition on its part of the need for genuine partnership with the voluntary sector. There is at present, according to some, a far from convincing attitude on the part of the Zonal administration to the goal of greater participation by the sector in development and program planning and other areas of importance. This, they thought needs to change. Despite the challenges and drawbacks, however, increased cooperation among NGOs working in Wollaita would enhance their effectiveness.

References

Action for Development (AFD). 2003. "Terminal" Report on Integrated Community Development in North Omo (Community Development and SACCO Promotion). Wolayta Soddo, December.

_____. 2004. Terminal Evaluation of the Integrated Community Development and Saving and Credit Cooperative Promotion Project in Wolaita and Gamo Goffa Zones (SNNPRG) (2000-2003). Addis Ababa, April.

_____. 2005. Integrated Community Development in North Omo Project. Consolidation Phase (Jan. 2004-Nov. 2005). Project Terminal Report. Addis Ababa, December.

Bush, Jennifer. 2002. Baseline Report. Household Food Economy Assessment. Boloso Sore Woreda, Wolayita Zone, SNNPR. Addis Ababa, Christian Aid/ ICCO-Netherlands.

Byrne, Peter V. 1981. Wollaita Agricultural Development Unit, Future Programme Proposal. Nairobi, October.

Carswell, Grace et al. 1999. *Sustainable Livelihoods in Southern Ethiopia*. IDS Research Report 44. Brighton, Sussex: Institute of Development Research.

Central Statistical Authority (CSA). 1996. *The 1994 Population and Housing Census of Ethiopia: Results for Southern Nations, Nationalities and Peoples' Region*. Addis Ababa, June.

Christian Relief and Development Association (CRDA) and Disaster Prevention and Preparedness Commission (DPPC). 2004. Information Package on NGO Contributions. Development Studies Associates, Addis Ababa, March.

Dagnew Eshete. 1995a. Food Shortages and Household Coping Strategies by Income Groups: A Case Study of Wolaita District in Southern Ethiopia. In *Ethiopian Agriculture: Problems of Transformation. Proceedings of the Fourth Annual Conference on the Ethiopian Economy*, edited by Dejene Aredo and Mulat Demeke. Addis Ababa: Ethiopian Economic Association.

_____. 1995b. Differential Socio-economic Impact of Food Shortages and Household Coping Strategies: A Case Study of Wolaita District in Southern Ethiopia. *Africa Development*, Vol. XX, No. 1.

_____. 1995c. Indigenous Coping Mechanisms in Times of Disaster: A Case Study of Wolaita Awraja in Southern Ethiopia. Paper presented at the Regional Workshop on the Lessons Learnt and Future Development Priorities and Strategies 10 Years after the 1984/85 Famine, Awassa, 27-28 February.

Department of Agriculture and Rural Development (DARD). 2006. Information from its files. Soddo.

Department of Finance and Economic Development (DFED). 2005. Zonal Basic Socio-Economic and Demographic Information. Wolaita Soddo. ABC Printing Press.

_____. 2005b. Workshop on Zonal Population Program (1998-2000 Eth C). Soddo, June.

_____. 2006. Information from its files. Soddo.

Department of Trade, Industry and Urban Development. 2006. Information from its files. Soddo.

Dessalegn Rahmato. 1992. *The Dynamics of Rural Poverty: Case Studies from a District in Southern Ethiopia.* Monograph Series 2/92. Dakar: CODESRIA.

_____. 1995. Resilience and Vulnerability: Enset Agriculture in Southern Ethiopia. *Journal of Ethiopian Studies*, Vol. XXVIII, No. 1.

_____. 2003. *Resettlement in Ethiopia: The Tragedy of Population Relocation in the 1980s.* FSS Discussion Paper No. 11, Forum for Social Studies, Addis Ababa.

DTRC/IDR. 1998. Southern Nations, Nationalities and Peoples Region. Community and Family Survey: 1997. Addis Ababa University and Brown University.

Ethiopian Economic Association/Ethiopian Economic Policy Research Institute (EEA/EEPRI). 2006. *Evaluation of the Ethiopian Agricultural Extension with Particular Emphasis on the Participatory Demonstration and Training Extension System (PADETES).* March. Addis Ababa: EEA/EEPRI.

Elton, A. 1967. A Report on the Feasibility of an Agricultural Settlement Project in Wollamo Sub-Province of Sidam Province, Ethiopia. [Unpublished report] ECA/FAO Joint Agriculture Division, Addis Ababa.

Eyasu Elias. 2000. Soil Enrichment and Depletion in Southern Ethiopia. In *Nutrients on the Move: Soil Fertility Dynamics in African Farming Systems,* edited by T. Hilhorst and F. Muchena. London: IIED.

_____. 2002. *Farmers' Perception of Soil Fertility Change and Management.* Addis Ababa: SOS-Sahel and Institute for Sustainable Development.

Family Guidance Association (FGA). 2006. Information from its files. Soddo.

FARM Africa. 2001. Farmer Participatory Research in Southern Ethiopia. The Experiences of the Farmers' Research Project. London: FARM Africa.

Food and Agriculture Organization (FAO). 1998. NGO Programme of Support for Local Agricultural Rehabilitation Initiatives. Ethiopia Project Findings and Recommendation. Rome: FAO.

Federal Democratic Republic of Ethiopia (FDRE). 2001. *Policies, Strategies and Approaches to Rural Development* [Amharic]. Addis Ababa: Ministry of Information.

Gezahegn Ayele et al. 2006. Water Harvesting Practices and Impacts on Livelihood Outcomes in Ethiopia. Ethiopian Development Research Institute, Addis Ababa, June.

Mellese Madda. 2005. Promises, Expectations and Realities of Resettlement: The Dynamics of Intra-Zonal Resettlement in Walayta of Southern Ethiopia. MA Thesis, Department of Social Anthropology, Addis Ababa University.

Ministry of Agriculture. 1973. Wollamo Agricultural Development Unit Program. Phase II Project Proposal, Volume I and II.

New Coalition for Food Security in Ethiopia (NCFSE). 2003. Food Security Programme. Addis Ababa, November.

Transitional Government of Ethiopia. 1993. Population Policy. Addis Ababa.

Tsedeke Abate et al. (eds). 1996. *Enset-Based Sustainable Agriculture in Ethiopia*. Addis Ababa: Institute of Agricultural Research.

Wollaita Agricultural Development Unit, (WADU). 1974. Annual Report- July 8, 1973-July 7, 1974. WADU Publication No. 41, Soddo.

_____. 1975. Annual Report 1974-75. WADU Publication No. 42. Soddo.

_____. 1976a. General Agricultural Survey of Bele (Koysha Lowland). WADU Publication No. 45, Soddo.

_____. 1976b. Agricultural Survey of Bolosso 1971. WADU Publication No. 48, Soddo.

_____. 1976c. Annual Report 1975-76. WADU Publication No 51. Soddo.

_____. 1976d. 1976 General Agricultural Survey Report. WADU Publication No. 58, Soddo.

_____. 1979a. Agronomic Report 1977/78 and 1978/79. WADU Publication No. 62, Soddo.

_____. 1979b. Annual Crop Sample Survey 1977/78. WADU Publication No. 63, Soddo.

_____. 1982. Annual Report 1980/81. WADU Publication. Soddo.

_____. 1983. Annual Report 1981/82. WADU Publication. Soddo.

Wolaita Development Association. 2003. First Strategic Review and Planning Exercise. Draft Final Report. Addis Ababa, May.

Annex 1

NGO Officers, Local Officials and Businesspersons Interviewed

The following persons were interviewed for this study in September and October 2006. They are listed in the order in which the interview was held. The place where the interview took place is shown in brackets.

Dejazmatch Woldesemayat Gebrewold (Addis Ababa)
Former Governor of Wollamo Awraja

Kifle Lemma (Addis Ababa)
Humanitarian Program Coordinator, OXFAM GB

Kebede Molla (Addis Ababa)
OXFAM GB

Debela Dinka (Addis Ababa)
Former Employee of WADU

Amare Kebede (Addis Ababa)
Former Employee of WADU

Zerihun Beyene (Addis Ababa)
Deputy National Director, World Vision

Berkako Iguma (Addis Ababa)
Director, Central Branch, World Vision

Kukura Waffo (Addis Ababa)
Director, Southern Branch, World Vision

Fekadu Beza (Soddo)
Head, Department of Finance and Economic Development

Datta Dergasso (Soddo)
Former Administrator of Bolosso woreda

Paulos Mojjo (Soddo)
Head, Omo Microfinance

Defabachew Selegn (Soddo)
Family Guidance Association

Geremew Haileyessus (Soddo)
Africa Humanitarian Action

Dessalegn Tanga (Soddo)
Former Employee of WADU

Altaye Ayele (Soddo)
Manager, Wollaita Development Association

Mengistu Arba (Soddo)
Head, Planning and Programming, Wollaita Development Association

Eyessus Chute (Soddo)
Head, Wisdom Microfinance

Ammanuel Jarso (Soddo)
Food Security Desk, Dept of Agriculture and Rural Development

Melkamu Tadesse (Soddo)
Head, Department of Agriculture and Rural Development

Berhanu Manna (Soddo)
Local Businessman

Zerfu Atnafu (Soddo)
Head, Department of Trade, Industry and Urban Development

Wasse Alemu (Soddo)
Investment Desk, Dept of Trade, Industry and Urban Development

Tegegn Arasho (Soddo)
Micro-enterprise Desk, Dept of Trade, Industry and Urban Development

Densasa Regassa (Soddo)
Head, Soddo Zuria ADP, World Vision

Takele Aiza (Soddo)
Local Businessman

Tamrat Wondimu (Soddo)
   Local Businessman

Yoseph Negassa (Addis Ababa)
   Executive Director, Action for Development

Feyera Ahmad (Addis Ababa)
   Manager, SOS-Sahel

Peasants Interviewed

In Damot Gale Woreda
    Setta Gagabo
    Serango Tema
    Kemal Arebo
    Getachew Bogale
    Abdurahman Adebo

In Bolosso Woreda
    Sappa Sakalo
    Matewos Tulam
    Goshem Setta
    Yohannes Gadebo
    Ayele Tanga

In Kindo Koysha Woreda
    Taddesse Tebaro
    Bergene Bafta
    Zerihun Bachere
    Gua Motelo
    Harbero Dabento

Annex 2: Map of Wollaita

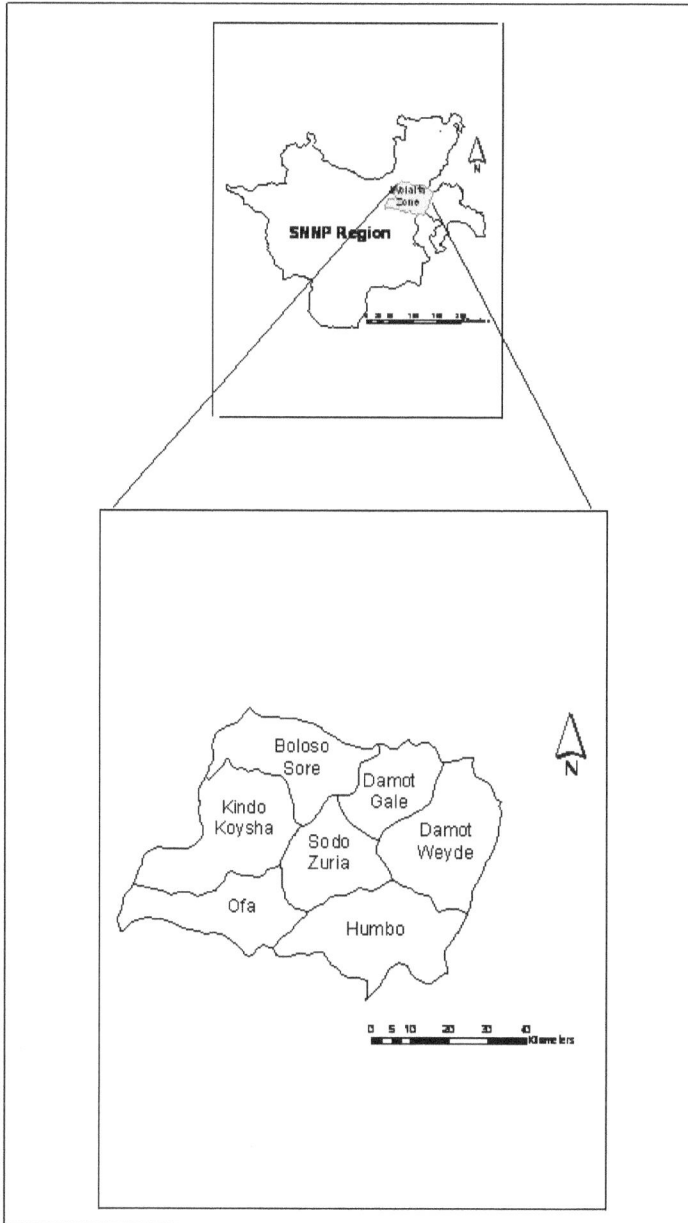

www.ingramcontent.com/pod-product-compliance
Lightning Source LLC
Chambersburg PA
CBHW051426290326
41932CB00048B/3234